# ECCE ROMANI

**A Latin Reading Course**
**Prepared by The Scottish Classics Group**

## 4
# Pastimes
# and Ceremonies

*Second Edition*

# Oliver & Boyd

# Contents

# 42
# At the Baths

One of the main entertainments of the Roman was his daily visit to the baths, either to the public **thermae** or to the smaller, private **balneae**. He would expect to find three basic rooms—a warm room (**tepidarium**) which he would enter after undressing in the changing-room (**apodyterium**); a hot room (**caldarium**) where hot water would be provided in a specially heated room which might also incorporate a steam bath; and a cold room (**frigidarium**) where he could plunge into a cold bath after the heat of the **caldarium**. To clean himself, the Roman would have himself rubbed down with oil (**unguentum**) which was then scraped off with a special metal instrument (**strigilis**). He would also expect to find an exercise-ground (**palaestra**), often in the open air, with a covered portico round it, where he could take exercise by playing with a ball (**pila ludere**), by wrestling (**luctari**), by fencing at a post (**palus**) or by weight-lifting. There was a great variety of ball games including **harpastum**, a game involving the "snatching" (**rapere**) of a heavy ball, and **trigon**, a throwing and catching game played by three people. At the end of it all he would be rubbed down with a towel (**linteum**). The baths were regarded as a social club, and people went there to exercise, play games and meet each other, as well as to wash.

iam hora sexta erat. Titus Cornelius, ut cotidie solebat, domo egressus, in Campum Martium ad Thermas Neroneas descendit, nam eo amici eius conveniebant et de rebus urbanis colloquebantur.

quo cum Titus pervenisset, pecunia data, in vestibulum ingressus est. ibi complures ex amicis eum salutaverunt atque una in apodyterium inierunt. vestimenta exuta tradiderunt servis suis, qui unguenta et strigiles portabant.

iam uncti in palaestram exierunt ubi multi cives variis modis se exercebant. alii harpastum rapiebant, alii trigone ludebant, alii luctabantur, alii palum gladio petebant. Titus cum duobus amicis trigone ludebat. cum satis se ita exercuissent, a servis plus unguenti poposcerunt et strigilibus defricti sunt. mox tepidarium, deinde caldarium inierunt. hic, cum calorem et vaporem vix pati possent, haud multum morabantur. cum in tepidarium regressi essent, statim inde frigidarium intraverunt et in aquam frigidam desiluerunt. postea linteis tersi, vestimenta rursus induerunt.

ne tum quidem domum discesserunt sed, vino sumpto, inter se colloqui coeperunt. Titum, cum ille semper videretur omnia audivisse et vidisse, de rebus urbanis omnes rogabant. maxime enim cupiebant cognoscere quid in senatu ageretur, cur princeps ipse senatores omnes Romam arcessivisset, quae scelera liberti Caesaris admitterent.

"nil novi" respondit Titus, "sed heri in Balneis Palatinis rem ridiculam vidi; senex calvus, tunica russata indutus, inter pueros capillatos pila ludebat. eas pilas, quae ad terram ceciderant, non repetebat, nam servus follem habebat plenum pilarum quas ludentibus dabat. tandem hic senex digitos concrepuit et aquam poposcit. tum, cum manus lavisset, in capite unius ex pueris tersit!"

**eo,** there, to that place
**quo cum,** when ... there
**pecunia data,** after
   paying his entrance fee
**vestibulum, -i** (*n*),
   entrance passage
**vestimenta, -orum** (*n.pl*),
   clothes
**exerceo** (2), to exercise,
   train
**calor, caloris** (*m*), heat

**haud,** not
**postea,** afterwards
**vino sumpto,** after a drink
   of wine
**scelus, sceleris** (*n*), crime
**senex, senis** (*m*), old man
**calvus, -a, -um,** bald
**capillatus, -a, -um,**
   with long hair
**follis, follis** (*m*), bag
**digitus, -i** (*m*), finger

**exuo, exuere** (3), **exui, exutum,** to take off
**unguo, unguere** (3), **unxi, unctum,** to anoint, smear with oil
**defrico, defricare** (1), **defricui, defrictum,** to rub down
**tergeo, tergere** (2), **tersi, tersum,** to dry, wipe
**cognosco, cognoscere** (3), **cognovi, cognitum,** to find out, learn
**admitto, admittere** (3), **admisi, admissum,** to commit (a crime)
**repeto, repetere** (3), **repetivi, repetitum,** to pick up, recover
**concrepo, concrepare** (1), **concrepui,** to snap (the fingers)

A bronze oil flask and two strigils. (Reproduced by courtesy of the Trustees of the British Museum)

# VERBS: Subjunctive Mood

Look at these sentences:

piratae rogabant qui **essemus**, unde **venissemus**, quo iter **faceremus**.
*The pirates kept asking who we were, where we had come from and where we were travelling.*

cum se **exercuissent**, in tepidarium ingressi sunt.
*When they had exercised, they went into the warm room.*

nocte, cum omnes **dormirent**, ego surrexi.
*At night, since they were all sleeping, I got up.*

cum navis in insulam ventis **acta esset**, nos in terram evasimus.
*When the ship had been driven on to the island by the winds, we escaped ashore.*

The verbs in bold type are examples of the *subjunctive mood* which frequently occurs in Latin in subordinate clauses.

7

## Imperfect Tense

This is formed from the present active infinitive by the addition of the person endings:

*Active*

| Group 1 | Group 2 | Group 3 | Group 4 | esse |
|---------|---------|---------|---------|------|
| portarem | moverem | mitterem | audirem | essem |
| portares | moveres | mitteres | audires | esses |
| portaret | moveret | mitteret | audiret | esset |
| portaremus | moveremus | mitteremus | audiremus | essemus |
| portaretis | moveretis | mitteretis | audiretis | essetis |
| portarent | moverent | mitterent | audirent | essent |

*Passive*

| | | | |
|---------|---------|---------|---------|
| portarer | moverer | mitterer | audirer |
| portareris | movereris | mittereris | audireris |
| portaretur | moveretur | mitteretur | audiretur |
| portaremur | moveremur | mitteremur | audiremur |
| portaremini | moveremini | mitteremini | audiremini |
| portarentur | moverentur | mitterentur | audirentur |

Compare **essem, possem, vellem, nollem, mallem, irem.**

## Pluperfect Tense

The *active* is made up of the perfect active infinitive plus the person endings.

The *passive* is made up in the same way as the indicative passive, but **essem** is substituted for **eram.**

| *Active* |
|----------|
| audivissem |
| audivisses |
| audivisset |
| audivissemus |
| audivissetis |
| audivissent |

| *Passive* |
|-----------|
| auditus essem |
| auditus esses |
| auditus esset |
| auditi essemus |
| auditi essetis |
| auditi essent |

The examples of the subjunctive you have met so far have been in subordinate clauses beginning with **cum** (when, since) or a question word. Here, the subjunctive is translated into English as the corresponding tense of the indicative.

## Exercise 42a

*Translate:*

1  piratae rogabant quis esset meus dominus et quo iret.
2  cum nollem dominum relinquere, conatus sum eum servare.
3  cum prima luce profecti essemus, iam defessi eramus.
4  ludi magister rogavit unde Aeneas venisset et quo navigare in animo haberet.
5  cum multos annos navigavissemus, tandem ad Italiam pervenimus.
6  grammaticus me rogavit quando domo abiissem.
7  mater filium rogavit cur iratus esset.
8  cum diu ambulavissent, defessi erant.
9  cum lupum conspexissem, quam celerrime aufugi.
10  ego nesciebam cur Romam proficisceremur.

The women's changing-room (**apodyterium**) of the baths at Herculaneum. (Photograph, the Mansell Collection)

# The Baths

In addition to the many references to baths in Roman literature, much information about the **balneae** and **thermae** can be deduced from the archaeological remains of bathing establishments still evident today. In Rome, the great Thermae of Diocletian now house the National Museum, its extensive grounds having been laid out by Michelangelo centuries after the baths were built; and grand opera is performed during the summer months in the Baths of Caracalla.

At Pompeii, both public and private bathing establishments have been found, and even in many of the houses there are full suites of bathrooms—warm, hot and cold rooms—which were apparently used only by the family. On country estates and in town houses, in addition to the suites of baths for the owner, there were bath houses for slaves.

The first public baths in Rome were built in the second century BC and they were small, practical wash-houses for men

Reconstruction of baths at Chesters

Key:
A    Changing room      F    Hot bath
B    Hot dry room       G    Second warm room
C    Latrine            H    Hot room
D    Cold room          I    First warm room
E    Third warm room    J    Boiler
                        K    Stoke-hole

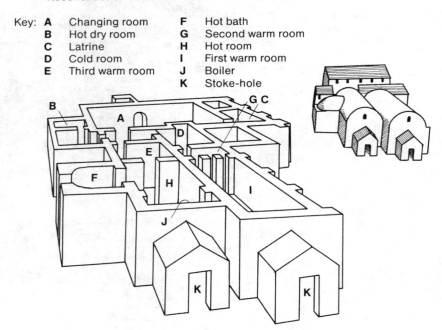

only. Later, bathing establishments called **balneae** began to be built at private expense and run for profit by individuals or a consortium. As the practice of bathing became more and more popular, huge baths (**thermae**) were built by the State. These were increased in size and splendour under the emperors, e.g. the Thermae of Caracalla (AD 217) and of Diocletian (AD 303).

Romans of all social classes could spend an hour or more in the luxury of such complexes for only a **quadrans**, the smallest Roman coin. Children were admitted free. The management of the state **thermae** was awarded for a fixed sum to a contractor. Sometimes a rich citizen or magistrate undertook to pay him the equivalent of the total entrance fees for a certain period, during which entry to the baths was entirely free.

So attached were the Romans to their daily hot steam-bath that they built baths in most communities throughout their Empire. Where there were hot springs, as in Bath, England, they used these and built gymnasia and dressing-rooms around them. Where there were no hot springs, they heated the air by "hypocausts", a system whereby hot air from a furnace

The "Hunting Baths" on the outskirts of Leptis Magna, North Africa. (Photograph, Miss G. Farnell)

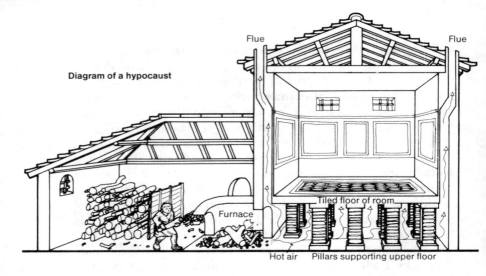

Diagram of a hypocaust

Flue

Flue

Tiled floor of room

Furnace

Hot air

Pillars supporting upper floor

circulated under the raised floor and through ducts and vents in the walls. The fuel for the furnace, which was stoked by slaves, was wood and charcoal. Huge reservoirs were built near the baths to provide a constant and plentiful supply of water.

In Rome, the baths opened at noon and remained open till dusk. The opening and closing times were indicated by the striking of a gong.

Many establishments had separate facilities for men and women bathers; others fixed different hours for the two sexes. Mixed bathing, however, was usual in the open-air swimming pools that formed part of the larger baths. Ladies who cared for their reputation did not frequent the baths.

Bathers would take various articles with them to the baths, including towels, bottles of oil and strigils. All but the poor would bring their own slaves to attend them, but it was possible to hire the services of others at the baths (e.g. masseur, barber). Attendants would guard clothes for a small fee.

Roman baths varied considerably in size and layout, but in all of them the following series of rooms was to be found:

1 **apodyterium:** a changing room with stone benches and rows of deep holes in the walls for holding clothes.
2 **frigidarium:** cold room, with cold plunge bath at one side.
3 **tepidarium:** warm room, to acclimatise bathers to the difference in temperature between the cold and hot rooms.
4 **caldarium:** hot room, with hot bath and hot air like the modern Turkish bath. It was the best-lit room and was equipped with basins and tubs.

In addition, some baths had a "Spartan" room (**Laconicum**) where people sweated in dry heat as in a sauna. It had a dome on top with a round opening closed by a bronze disc on a chain. The bather could thus regulate the heat himself.

The bathers could take the three stages of bathing in any order, but it was usual to end up with a cold plunge. Medicinal and perfumed baths were also available.

The baths became a suitable place for taking exercise. A large complex would have a court for ball games and an area for gymnastics and wrestling, in addition to the swimming pool. There were various ball games, each using a different type of ball and sometimes a racquet as well. Hoops or a "dumb-bell" were also used for exercising.

The Roman baths were centres for recreation and relaxation in the fullest sense, and in the largest establishments the amenities could include gardens, reading-rooms and even libraries. "Snack-bars" (**popinae**) were numerous inside the building or near by, while vendors of every type advertised their wares on all sides.

**Plan of the Stabian Baths at Pompeii.**

Note that the women did not have a frigidarium. The hypocaust served both sections.

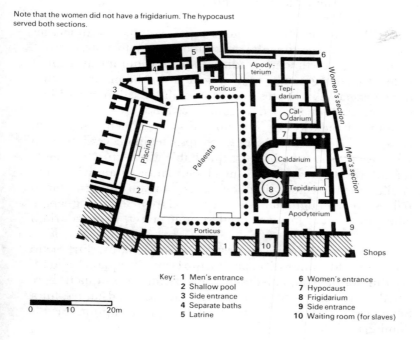

Key:
1 Men's entrance
2 Shallow pool
3 Side entrance
4 Separate baths
5 Latrine
6 Women's entrance
7 Hypocaust
8 Frigidarium
9 Side entrance
10 Waiting room (for slaves)

0    10    20m

13

# 43
# Stop Thief!

Marcus et Sextus e ludo egressi una cum Eucleide et altero servo domum ibant. subito Eucleides pueris "vultisne ad thermas ire?" inquit.

quibus verbis auditis, pueri maxime gaudebant. mox ad thermas advenerunt et in apodyterium intraverunt, quod iam erat plenum puerorum qui e ludo egressi eo cum paedagogis venerant. ibi vestimenta exuebant.

Marcus, vestimentis exutis, "nunc in palaestram exeamus" inquit. at Eucleides "minime!" inquit. "pater tuus me iussit vos ante nonam horam reducere." deinde alteri servo, cui nomen erat Asellus, "hic mane!" inquit. "vestimenta diligenter custodi! hic enim solent esse multi fures qui vestimenta surrepta in urbe vendunt."

Asellus respondit "ego semper vestimenta diligenter custodio. nemo vestimenta, me custode, surripere potest."

tum pueri, vestimentis traditis, in tepidarium intraverunt et inde in caldarium, ubi erat magna turba hominum. subito tamen exclamavit Sextus "aeger sum. hunc calorem pati non possum. exibo et ad apodyterium regrediar."

dum e tepidario exit, Asellum prope vestimenta sedentem conspexit. dormiebat Asellus. eo ipso tempore vestimenta a servo quodam surripiebantur. quod ubi vidit Sextus "prehende furem!" exclamavit. simul fur clamorem Sexti audivit, simul Asellus e sella exsiluit, simul Sextus ad ianuam cucurrit. fur in palaestram confugit, nam se in turba celare in animo habebat. cum tamen inde in viam evadere non posset, in frigidarium fugit.

Sextus tamen furem conspectum subsequebatur. fur, Sexto viso, iam valde timebat. in pavimento lapsus in aquam frigidam cecidit. statim in aquam desiluit Sextus. furem ex aqua trahere conabatur; sed frustra. cum tamen adiuvissent adstantes, fur a Sexto captus ex aqua extractus est. quem captum Sextus domino tradidit.

**quibus verbis auditis,**
   on hearing these words,
   when they heard this
**exeamus,** let us go out
**at,** but
**fur, furis** (*m*), thief

**me custode,** while I am
   on guard
**turba, -ae** (*f*), crowd
**pavimentum, -i** (*n*),
   tiled floor

**surripio, surripere** (3), **surripui, surreptum,** to steal
**prehendo, prehendere** (3), **prehendi, prehensum,** to seize
**exsilio, exsilire** (4), **exsilui,** to leap out
**confugio, confugere** (3), **confugi,** to flee for refuge
**subsequor, -sequi** (3), **-secutus sum** to follow up
**labor, labi** (3), **lapsus sum,** to slip

# VERBS: Participles III

You have already translated numerous examples of sentences
like

> **coquus vocatus** ab omnibus laudatus est.
> *The cook* **was summoned and** *was praised by all.*

where the perfect participle is translated by a main verb: "was
summoned and".

Similar participial phrases may appear in other cases, but the
meaning may be arrived at in exactly the same way. For
example,

1 Accusative:

> **coquum vocatum** omnes laudaverunt.
> *The cook* **was summoned and** *they all praised (him).*

2 Dative:

> **coquo vocato** omnes gratias egerunt.
> *The cook* **was summoned and** *they all gave thanks (to him).*

3 Ablative:

> **coquo vocato,** omnes cenam laudaverunt.
> *The cook* **was summoned and** *they all praised the dinner.*

The above technique will help you to establish the meaning of
the sentence, but it may not be in the most natural English.

There are several other ways of translating the same sentence, e.g. **coquum vocatum omnes laudaverunt** may be translated

> *The cook was summoned and they all praised him.*
> *When the cook was summoned, they all praised him.*
> *After the cook was summoned, they all praised him.*

or even actively

> *They all summoned the cook and praised him.*
> *Having summoned the cook, they all praised him.*
> *After summoning the cook, they all praised him.*

In the last sentence quoted on p. 15, the phrase **coquo vocato** is an example of the Latin construction *ablative absolute*, in which a noun (or pronoun) and a participle are in the ablative case, being neither subject (nominative), direct object (accusative), nor indirect object (dative) of the verb. An ablative absolute phrase is frequently separated from the rest of the sentence by a comma (or commas).

## Exercise 43a

*Translate:*

1. fur conspectus in palaestram celeriter cucurrit.
2. fure conspecto, Sextus magna voce clamavit.
3. Titus rogatus quid in senatu ageretur "nihil novi" respondit.
4. ludo confecto, in tepidarium intraverunt.
5. Titus somno excitatus ad Thermas ivit.
6. vestimentis Asello traditis, pueri in tepidarium inierunt.
7. vestimentis indutis, vinum sumpserunt.
8. strigilibus defricti tepidarium ingressi sunt.
9. Tito salutato, in apodyterium inierunt.
10. e ludo egressi pueri ad Thermas iverunt.

**conficio, conficere** (3), **confeci, confectum,** to finish

# Exercise 43b

*Translate:*

1  amici Titum conspectum salutaverunt.
2  vestimenta exuta servo tradita sunt.
3  vestimenta exuta Marcus servo tradidit.
4  vestimenta a servo accepta pueri induerunt.
5  ibi non diu morati in caldarium processerunt.
6  vino sumpto, inter se colloqui coeperunt.
7  in palaestram ingressi trigone ludebant.
8  Sextus Asellum dormientem conspexit.
9  Asello dormiente, fur vestimenta surripuit.
10 clamoribus adstantium perterritus fur effugere conatus est.

# Linking "qui"

In "Stop Thief!" you met the following phrases:

| | |
|---|---|
| **quibus** verbis auditis | *When they heard* **these** *words* |
| **cui** Asellus respondit | *Asellus replied* **to him** |
| **quod** ubi vidit | *When he saw* **this** |
| **quem** captum | *Now that he had caught* **him** |

This use of the relative pronoun at the beginning of a sentence provides a link with a person, thing or action in the previous sentence;

e.g. **quibus verbis** refers to what Eucleides said in the previous sentence.

**cui** refers to Eucleides who had just finished speaking.

**quod** refers to the theft Sextus had just seen.

**quem** refers to the thief mentioned in the previous sentence.

# 44
# Pyramus and Thisbe

In ancient Rome, the first contact which the public was likely to have with a new poem or a completed section of a longer poem would be, not through reading it in a book, but through listening to it at a public reading (**recitatio**) given by the poet in a private house or theatre or recital room. Some enterprising poets even tried to gather an audience at the public baths.

The love story of Pyramus and Thisbe, set in ancient Babylon and made familiar to English readers by Shakespeare's *A Midsummer Night's Dream*, was originally part of a long narrative poem called *Metamorphoses* by the Latin poet Ovid (43 BC–AD 17).

olim Babylone habitabat adulescens quidam pulcherrimus, nomine Pyramus. in vicina domo habitabat virgo cui nomen erat Thisbe. Pyramus hanc virginem in via forte conspectam statim amavit. et Thisbe, Pyramo viso, amore capta est. sed eheu! parentes et virginis et adulescentis, quoniam multos iam annos inter se rixabantur, eos convenire vetuerunt. Pyramo Thisben ne videre quidem licebat. valde dolebant et adulescens et virgo.

erat murus domui utrique communis. parva tamen rima, a nullo antea visa, ab amantibus inventa est. (quid non sentit amor?) quam ad rimam sedentes inter se secreto colloquebantur, alter alteri amorem exprimentes. sed mox, osculis muro datis, valedicebant inviti.

tandem novum consilium ceperunt. constituerunt enim, parentibus insciis, e domo nocte exire, in silvam convenire, sub arbore quadam considere. itaque Thisbe silentio noctis, cum vultum velamine celavisset, furtim egressa ad silvam festinavit. quo cum advenisset, sub illa arbore consedit. ecce tamen venit leo saevus, ore sanguine bovis asperso. quo conspecto, Thisbe perterrita in speluncam, quae prope erat, confugit. et dum fugit, velamen reliquit. quod velamen leo ore sanguineo rapuit, sed mox deposuit.

haud multo post Pyramus ex urbe egressus, dum ad arborem eandem progreditur, vestigia leonis vidit. subito puellae velamen sanguine aspersum conspexit. timore tremens "quid accidit?" clamavit. "eheu! ego te occidi, mea Thisbe, quod te iussi in silvam noctu solam venire, nec prior veni. sine te vivere nolo." gladio igitur stricto, se vulneravit atque ad terram cecidit moriens.

ecce! metu nondum deposito, Thisbe e spelunca timide exit, Pyramum quaerit. subito corpus eius humi iacens conspicit; multis cum lacrimis "Pyrame," clamat "quis hoc fecit?" deinde, suo velamine conspecto, iam moritura "o me miseram!" clamat. "velamen meum te perdidit. sine te vivere nolo." et gladio Pyrami ipsa se occidit.

parentes, dolore commoti, eos in eodem sepulcro sepeliverunt.

**virgo, virginis** (*f*), maiden
**forte,** by chance
**rixor** (1), to quarrel
**uterque, utraque, utrumque,** each (of two)
**rima, -ae** (*f*), crack
**osculum, -i** (*n*), kiss
**consilium, -i** (*n*), plan
**inscius, -a, -um,** not knowing
**vultus, -us** (*m*), face
**velamen, velaminis** (*n*), veil, shawl

**saevus, -a, -um,** fierce, savage
**ore sanguine asperso,** his mouth spattered with blood
**spelunca, -ae** (*f*), cave
**haud multo post,** not much later
**nec,** another form of **neque**
**prior, prioris,** first (of two)
**humi,** on the ground
**moritura,** intending to die, determined to die

**sentio, sentire** (4), **sensi, sensum,** to feel, notice
**exprimo, exprimere** (3), **expressi, expressum,** to express
**valedico, valedicere** (3), **valedixi, valedictum,** to say goodbye
**aspergo, aspergere** (3), **aspersi, aspersum,** to spatter, splash
**occido, occidere** (3), **occidi, occisum,** to kill
**vivo, vivere** (3), **vixi, victum,** to live
**perdo, perdere** (3), **perdidi, perditum,** to destroy

# VERBS: Participles IV

The following is a complete tabulation of the participles in Groups 1–4:

| Tense | Active | Passive |
|---|---|---|
| Present | 1 portans, portantis<br>   *carrying*<br>2 movens, moventis<br>   *moving*<br>3 mittens, mittentis<br>   *sending*<br>  faciens, facientis<br>   *doing, making*<br>4 audiens, audientis<br>   *hearing* | |
| Perfect | | 1 portatus, -a, -um<br>   (*having been*) *carried*<br>2 motus, -a, -um<br>   (*having been*) *moved*<br>3 missus, -a, -um<br>   (*having been*) *sent*<br>  factus, -a, -um<br>   (*having been*) *done, made*<br>4 auditus, -a, -um<br>   (*having been*) *heard* |
| Future | 1 portaturus, -a, -um<br>   *about to carry*<br>2 moturus, -a, -um<br>   *about to move*<br>3 missurus, -a, -um<br>   *about to send*<br>  facturus, -a, -um<br>   *about to make, do*<br>4 auditurus, -a, -um<br>   *about to hear* | |

## Notes

1 The present and future participles are active in meaning and form.

The perfect participle is passive in meaning and form.

2 The present participle of **ire** (*to go*) is **iens, euntis**.

3 The verb **esse** has no present participle. It is therefore necessary to supply the word "being" when translating certain ablative absolute phrases such as

**Caesare duce,** literally "Caesar (being) leader", i.e. "under Caesar's leadership"

**me custode,** literally "me (being) guard", i.e. "while I am on guard"

**inscia matre,** literally "mother (being) unaware", i.e. "without mother's knowledge".

4 Other possible translations of the future participle include: "going to", "likely to", "intending to", "determined to", "on the point of . . .ing".

Although the participles of deponent verbs have the same endings as the above, **all** the meanings are active:

| Present Participle | 1 conans, conantis, *trying* |
| | 2 pollicens, pollicentis, *promising* |
| | 3 sequens, sequentis, *following* |
| | 4 oriens, orientis, *rising* |
| Perfect Participle | 1 conatus, -a, -um, *having tried* |
| | 2 pollicitus, -a, -um, *having promised* |
| | 3 secutus, -a, -um, *having followed* |
| | 4 ortus, -a, -um, *having risen* |
| Future Participle | 1 conaturus, -a, -um, *about to try* |
| | 2 polliciturus, -a, -um, *about to promise* |
| | 3 secuturus, -a, -um, *about to follow* |
| | 4 oriturus, -a, -um, *about to rise* |

# Exercise 44a

*Translate:*

1  multis hominibus subsequentibus, fur effugere non potuit.
2  Sextus furem effugere conantem subsequebatur.
3  pueri calorem vix passi haud diu in caldario morabantur.
4  Sextus domum profecturus ab omnibus laudatus est.
5  Thisbe moritura ad terram cecidit.
6  Asello custode, vestimenta puerorum surrepta sunt.
7  Pyramus ad arborem illam progrediens vestigia leonis vidit.
8  velamine relicto, Thisbe in speluncam confugit.
9  ad rimam inter se secreto colloquentes amorem exprimebant.
10  Pyramus Thisben secuturus ex urbe profectus est.
11  sole oriente, mercatores profecti sunt ad Africam navigaturi.
12  multa virgini pollicitus, Pyramus ei valedixit.

# Exercise 44b

## Caesar visits Britain

*Translate:*

Gaius Iulius Caesar, dux praeclarus Romanorum, in Gallia pugnans multa de Britannia cognovit. mercatores enim ex Britannia ad Galliam transgressi multa emebant ac vendebant; et Britanni auxilium Gallis Caesari resistentibus semper mittebant. Caesar igitur, Gallis victis et navibus paratis, in Britanniam transgredi constituit. profecturi tamen milites, magna tempestate coorta, naves conscendere vix poterant. compluribus post diebus, cum tempestate naves paene deletae essent, Romani Britanniae appropinquantes incolas in omnibus collibus instructos conspexerunt. egredientes Romanos Britanni, pilis coniectis, depellere conati sunt; sed, quamquam multos Romanorum vulneraverunt, tandem superati sunt.

| | |
|---|---|
| **dux, ducis** (*m*), general | **instructus, -a, -um,** |
| **pugno** (1), to fight |   drawn up, deployed |
| **collis, collis** (*m*), hill | **pilum, -i** (*n*), javelin |

**vinco, vincere** (3), **vici, victum,** to conquer
**conscendo, conscendere** (3), **conscendi, conscensum,** to board
(ship)

# Exercise 44c

You have met most of the verbs listed on the left-hand side. Give the meanings of the compound verbs.

| | |
|---|---|
| **cedo** | procedo, incedo, praecedo, decedo, discedo, excedo |
| **mitto** | immitto, demitto, emitto, dimitto, admitto |
| **fero** | refero, profero, perfero, confero, affero, effero, praefero |
| **gradior** | transgredior, congredior, regredior, egredior, ingredior, progredior |
| **pono** | compono, impono, depono, expono, repono |
| **rumpo** | prorumpo, irrumpo, erumpo |
| **iacio** | inicio, abicio, eicio, conicio, deicio |
| **duco** | educo, introduco, deduco, reduco, induco, traduco |

# The Early Emperors of Rome

| | |
|---|---|
| Augustus | 27 BC–AD 14 |
| Tiberius | AD 14–37 |
| Caligula | AD 37–41 |
| Claudius | AD 41–54 |
| Nero | AD 54–68 |
| Year of the Four Emperors (Galba, Otho, Vitellius, Vespasian) | AD 68–69 |
| Vespasian | AD 69–79 |
| Titus | AD 79–81 |
| Domitian | AD 81–96 |
| Nerva | AD 96–98 |
| Trajan | AD 98–117 |
| Hadrian | AD 117–138 |
| Antoninus Pius | AD 138–161 |
| Marcus Aurelius | AD 161–180 |

# 45
# A Rainy Day

Many of the games that children play today were also played by Roman children. They built toy houses and rode on long sticks; they had spinning tops, hoops which they bowled along with a stick, and dolls (**pupae**); they tossed coins, calling out "heads or a ship" (**capita aut navia**); and they played at being soldiers or judges or consuls. They also used to harness mice to toy carts.

Nuts (**nuces**) were used in several games. One nut was balanced on three others and children competed at knocking them down with a fruit stone. The winner got all the nuts. They also competed at throwing nuts into a narrow-necked vase which had been placed some distance away from them. A very popular game was to ask your partner to guess whether the number of nuts or pebbles or other similar objects which you had in your hand was odd or even (**par impar**). Another popular game played with the hands was **micatio**. Two players each showed a number of fingers on their right hands (**digitis micare**) and simultaneously called out how many fingers altogether they believed had been shown. The round was won by the player who first guessed correctly five times. The game is still played in modern times in Italy under the name of **morra**.

Both adults and children played a game which resembled draughts and chess (**ludus latrunculorum**) in which they moved two sets of pieces on a chequered board.

Older children and young men took exercise on the Campus Martius—wrestling, riding, driving chariots—followed possibly by a swim across the Tiber.

"eheu!" mussavit Marcus. "cur 'eheu'?" rogavit Sextus.

"semper pluit!" respondit Marcus. "ego in animo habebam ad Campum Martium hodie descendere et ad palaestram ire, sed pater nos domi manere iussit. puto patrem esse crudelem."

eo ipso tempore Eucleides ingressus pueros rogavit cur tam tristes essent. "in palaestram ire cupiebamus" inquit Marcus, "sed pater hoc vetuit."

cui Eucleides "bono animo este!" inquit. "ego vos docebo latrunculis ludere. puto hunc ludum esse optimum."

duas fere horas ita ludebant. postremo Sextus exclamavit "hic ludus me non iam delectat. ego puto hunc ludum esse pessimum. age, Marce! nonne vis par impar ludere vel digitis micare?"

statim clamare coeperunt ambo. simul Marcus "quinque!", simul Sextus "novem!" deinde Marcus "octo!", Sextus "sex!"

"tacete, pueri!" interpellavit Eucleides. "nolite clamoribus vestris vexare matrem et Corneliam! puto vos esse molestissimos hodie." at pueri ei non parebant. itaque Cornelia, clamoribus auditis, in atrium ingressa rogavit quid facerent.

"noli nos vexare!" inquit Sextus. "abi! sed cur pupam in manibus habes? num pupa ludis?"

"stultus es, Sexte! pupa non est mea. num credis me pupa ludere? hanc pupam, quam ego ipsa feci, filiae Davi dono dabo. hodie est dies natalis eius."

subito Sextus, pupa abrepta, in peristylium aufugit. quo viso, Eucleides Sexto clamavit. "noli pupam laedere! statim eam refer!"

eo ipso tempore ingressus est Cornelius. cum audivisset quid Sextus fecisset, "Sexte!" clamavit. "veni huc!" puer, iam timidus, in atrium regressus pupam Corneliae reddidit. tum Cornelius Sextum secum ex atrio eduxit.

quo facto, Marcus rogavit "quid pater faciet? quid Sexto fiet?"

cui Cornelia "puto" inquit "patrem in animo habere Sextum verberare."

---

**puto** (1), I think, consider
**bono animo es (este)!**
  Cheer up!
**ludus, -i** (*m*), game
**fere,** almost, approximately
**postremo,** finally
**ambo,** both
**vester, vestra,**
  **vestrum,** your

**pareo** (2) ( + *dat.*), to obey
**pupa, -ae** (*f*), doll
**num?** surely . . . not?
**dono dare,** to give as a gift
**dies natalis,** birthday
**peristylium, -i** (*n*), peristyle
**quid Sexto fiet?** What
  will become of Sextus?

---

**laedo, laedere** (3), **laesi, laesum,** to harm

# Accusative and Infinitive I

In Story 45 the following sentences occurred:

| | |
|---|---|
| puto **hunc ludum esse** optimum. | *I think* **that this game is** *a very good one.* |
| puto **vos esse** molestissimos. | *I think* **that you are** *very annoying.* |
| num credis **me** pupa **ludere?** | *Surely you do not believe* **that I am playing** *with a doll?* |

In such sentences, you are being given two pieces of information:

(1) I think      (2) what I think

    **puto**         **hunc ludum esse optimum.**
         *that*    *this game is a very good one.*

You will see that, in the second part, the Latin subject is expressed in the *accusative* case and the verb is in the *infinitive*, where English says "that this game" and "is".

Similarly,

**scio**         **vos esse molestissimos.**
*I know*   *that*   *you are very troublesome.*

**videmus**     **Davum in agris laborare.**
*We see*   *that*   *Davus is working in the fields.*

**audio**       **eum domi morari.**
*I hear*   *that*   *he is staying at home.*

Other verbs which may be followed by the *accusative and infinitive* construction include **dico** (I say), **spero** (I hope), **sentio** (I feel).

In translating this Latin construction, the next English word after verbs such as "I think", "I know", "I believe" will most often be "that".

**nuces relinquere,** *to leave childhood behind* (Can you think why the phrase has this meaning?)

26

# Exercise 45a

*Translate:*

1 Eucleides dicit ludum latrunculorum esse optimum.
2 scio Cornelium esse senatorem Romanum.
3 nos omnes scimus Corneliam esse puellam Romanam.
4 puto Sextum puerum temerarium esse.
5 audio Cornelium ad Curiam festinare.
6 scit ancillas cenam parare.
7 video haud longam esse viam.
8 audio cauponem esse amicum Eucleidis.
9 putamus in agris laborare servos.
10 credo Aureliam ad urbem proficisci.
11 dicunt Marcum dormire.
12 scimus semper esurire pueros.
13 audio Titum mappam non habere.
14 Cornelia putat pupam esse pulcherrimam.


# Exercise 45b

*Select and translate:*

1 alii putant (Sextus/Sextum) esse bonum, alii putant eum (est/erat/esse) molestum.
2 Davus quidem scit omnes (pueros/puerum/pueri) saepe esse (molestum/molesti/molestos).
3 at Aurelia putat Marcum et Sextum semper bonos (sunt/esse/erant).
4 Sextus Marco dicit Davum (esse/est/sum) iracundum.
5 semper respondet Marcus (Davi/Davo/Davum) non (esse/est) iracundum.
6 dicit Davum in agris diligenter (laborare/laboravit/laborat).
7 Sextus respondet Davum sub arbore cotidie post meridiem (dormis/dormiebat/dormire).
8 Cornelia putat (pueri/pueris/pueros) haud diligenter (laboraverunt/laborant/laborare).
9 dicit Cornelia Marcum et (Sexti/Sextum/Sextus) saepe in lecto diu (iacere/iacent/iacemus).
10 Flavia, amica Corneliae, putat (Cornelia/Corneliam/Corneliae) puellam pulcherrimam (esse/sunt/est).

# Exercise 45c

*Study this example:*
> Davus est iracundus.
> quid dicis?
> dico Davum esse iracundum.

*Following the above pattern, complete these examples:*
1 Sextus est puer temerarius.
   quid dicis?
   dico . . . .
2 pater Marci est crudelis.
   quid putat Sextus?
   Sextus putat . . . .
3 Cornelius est senator Romanus.
   quid dicitis?
   dicimus . . . .
4 adstantes furem ex aqua extrahunt.
   quid dicis?
   dico adstantes . . . .
5 puer exclamat "calorem pati non possum."
   quid exclamat puer?
   exclamat se . . . .

# Exercise 45d

*Using Story 45 as a guide, translate into Latin:*
1 Eucleides thinks that this is a very good game.
2 Eucleides thinks that the boys are very annoying today.
3 Do you believe that Cornelia is playing with a doll?
4 Cornelia believes that her father intends to beat Sextus.
5 Eucleides thinks that the boys are annoying Cornelia with their shouts.

**morituri te salutant,** *Those who are about to die salute you.*
(How the gladiators in the arena hailed their emperor.)

# Circus and Arena

The Romans did not have regular sporting events as we have at weekends, or organised entertainment available every day as we have in the theatre or cinema. Instead, to celebrate religious festivals, commemorate great national victories or honour the emperor, there were public holidays. These lasted a varying number of days, during which entertainments were presented. The number of these festivals increased as time went on until, by the reign of Claudius, 159 days of the year were holidays.

Admission to the shows was free and all the emperors made sure there was plenty of entertainment. According to Fronto:

> Trajan sensibly always paid attention to the idols of the theatre, the circus or the arena because he knew that the entertainment of the people was very important to the government; doling out corn or money might keep individuals quiet, but shows were necessary to keep the mob happy.

Juvenal too refers to the demand of the Roman mob for **panem et circenses** — the bread-dole and games in the Circus.

The cost of the public games was met by the State. Often magistrates added to the grant from their own pockets in order to increase their own popularity and therefore their chance of success in their careers. To do this they even ran into debt:

> Julius Caesar spent money so recklessly that many thought he was paying a high price to create a short-lived sensation, but really he was buying very cheaply the most powerful position in the world. Before entering politics he was thirteen hundred talents in debt. As aedile he staged games with 320 pairs of gladiators fighting in single combat. In this and his other extravagance in presenting theatrical performances, processions and public banquets, he completely outdid all previous efforts to obtain publicity in this way.
>
> Plutarch, *Caesar 5*

# Chariot Racing

The most popular attractions were spectacles in the amphitheatre and chariot-racing. You have read about chariot-
racing in the Circus Maximus in Chapter 27, Book 2.

The excitement, danger and betting ensured its popularity
with almost everyone—but not with Pliny the Younger:

> The races were on—a type of entertainment which does not appeal
> to me, as I find no novelty or variety in it. To have seen it once is
> enough. Therefore I am all the more astonished that so many
> thousand grown men should have this childish passion for watching
> over and over again horses galloping and drivers standing in
> chariots. There would be some sense in it if they went to see the
> speed of the horses or the skill of the drivers; but in fact it is the
> colours they support. If the colours were changed in mid-race, they
> would change their support and quickly desert those horses and
> drivers whom they recognise in the distance and whose names they
> chant.
>
> Pliny, *Epistles IX. 6*

Some of the emperors, however, held very different views:

> Chariot-racing was Nero's passion from his early years and he was
> always talking about the races even when he was told not to. On one
> occasion, he was bemoaning to his fellow pupils the fate of a
> "Green" driver who had been dragged by his horses, when his tutor
> scolded him. Nero pretended that he had been discussing the fate of
> Hector.
>
> At the beginning of his reign he played every day with ivory
> chariots on a board. He came back to town for all the races, even for
> unimportant meetings. Everyone knew on which days Nero would
> be in town. He made it quite obvious that he wanted the number of
> prizes increased. As a result there were more race meetings and they
> continued until a late hour. Soon Nero himself wanted to drive in
> open competition. He had a practice run in his gardens before an
> audience of slaves and riff-raff. Then he put himself on view in the
> Circus Maximus, with one of his freedmen dropping the napkin
> from the position the magistrate usually occupied.
>
> Suetonius, *Nero 22*

In order to get through 100 races in one day, Domitian reduced the number of laps from seven to five.

Suetonius, Domitian 4

Caligula was such a keen fan of the "Green" team that he frequently dined and even spent the night in their quarters. At a party he gave the driver Eutychus two million sesterces in gifts. The day before the races he used to send his soldiers to order silence in the neighbourhood, so that the horse Incitatus should not be disturbed. This horse had a marble stall, an ivory manger, purple blankets and a collar of precious stones, as well as a house, a retinue of slaves and furniture so that guests invited in his name could be entertained with proper elegance. Caligula is also said to have intended making Incitatus a consul.

Suetonius, Caligula 55

The driver of a four-horse chariot passing the winning-post. (Photograph, Michael Holford)

# 46
# Looking Forward to the Games

postridie, dum Gaius Cornelius in tablino scribit, subito intravit
Titus, frater eius.

"salve, Gai!" clamavit Titus. "quid agis?"

"bene!" respondit Cornelius. "sed semper sum, ut vides,
negotiosus."

cui Titus "pro certo habeo te cras non laboraturum esse.
omnes enim cives Romani ad munera ituri sunt. spero te
quoque ad munera iturum esse."

at Cornelius "munera?" inquit. "quid dicis, mi Tite?"

"pro di immortales!" exclamavit Titus. "cras Caesar amphitheatrum aperiet novum. tu tamen rogas quid dicam!"

Cornelius autem cum risu "nonne sentis me per iocum hoc
dixisse? certe hic dies maxime omnium memorabilis erit.
constat Iudaeos diligenter laboravisse et amphitheatrum
summa celeritate confecisse. nos templum illorum delevimus,
illi amphitheatrum aedificaverunt nostrum."

cui Titus "mehercule! totum populum continebit hoc
amphitheatrum. cras mane viae erunt plenae hominum qui ab
omnibus partibus ad spectaculum congredientur."

"ita!" inquit Cornelius. "puto tamen Aureliam eo non
ituram esse. scis enim Aureliam neque munera neque sangui-
nem amare. Aurelia domi manere mavult. Marcum tamen
mecum sum ducturus. iam adulescens est et mox togam virilem
sumet. Sextus autem, quod adhuc puer est, domi manebit;
nam, ut docet Seneca, 'quo maior populus, eo plus periculi.'
quota hora tu ad amphitheatrum cras mane es iturus?"

"prima luce" respondit Titus "nam mature advenire in
animo habeo. quando tu et Marcus eo pervenietis?"

"haud mature" inquit Cornelius, "sed pro certo habeo nos te
in amphitheatro visuros esse. nunc haec epistola est
conficienda. vale!"

"vale!" inquit Titus. "nos abituri te salutamus!"

**postridie,** next day
**negotiosus, -a, -um,** busy
**pro certo habeo,** I am sure
**munera, munerum**
 (*n.pl*), games
**spero** (1), to hope
**pro di immortales!**
 Good heavens!

**constat,** it is agreed
**Iudaei, Iudaeorum** (*m.pl*), Jews
**mavult,** (she) prefers
**quo maior . . ., eo plus . . .,**
 the greater . . ., the more . . .
**mature,** early
**epistola est conficienda,**
 the letter must be finished

**conficio, conficere** (3), **confeci, confectum,** to finish
**malo, malle, malui,** to prefer

# Accusative and Infinitive II

The future infinitive and the perfect infinitive also are used in this construction. Look at the following examples:

1 puto Aureliam eo non **ituram esse**.
 *I think that Aurelia* **will** *not* **go** *there.*

 pro certo habeo nos te **visuros esse**.
 *I am sure that we* **shall see** *you.*

 **ituram esse** and **visuros esse** are both *future infinitive active*. You will recognise this form as **esse** with the future participle, which appears in the accusative case agreeing with the subject of the infinitive clause in gender, case and number.

2 constat Iudaeos diligenter **laboravisse** et amphitheatrum summa celeritate **confecisse**.

 *It is agreed that the Jews* **have worked** *hard and* **finished** *the amphitheatre very quickly.*

 The *perfect infinitive active* (**laboravisse** and **confecisse**) can be recognised by the ending **-isse** (added to the perfect stem).

When **se** is used in the accusative and infinitive construction, it is translated as "he", "she" or "they" referring back to the subject of the verb of *saying, thinking, hearing,* etc., e.g.

 Titus dixit se ad amphitheatrum iturum esse.
 *Titus said that he would go to the amphitheatre.*

The use of **se** in this sentence shows that "he" refers to Titus. If the "he" had referred to someone else, **eum** would have been used instead of **se**.

33

puellae pueris dixerunt se eos adiuturas esse.
*The girls told the boys that they would help them.*

In this sentence **se** must refer to "the girls" and the future infinitive **adiuturas esse** is feminine accusative plural agreeing with **se**, while **eos** refers to "the boys".

## Exercise 46a

*Translate:*

1 putamus servos diligenter laboraturos esse.
2 scis Corneliam domi mansuram esse.
3 Cornelius putat Aureliam in peristylio ambulaturam esse.
4 scimus omnes cives Romanos ad munera ituros esse.
5 sperat Aurelia Cornelium domum festinaturum esse.
6 putasne patruum tuum ad amphitheatrum pervenisse?
7 constat illum diem memorabilem fuisse.
8 Cornelius audit Titum domum non venisse.
9 scimus Sextum ad patrem suum epistolam scripsisse.
10 audimus Caesarem amphitheatrum novum aperuisse.

## Exercise 46b

*Select the word which correctly completes the sense and translate:*

1 pro certo habeo puerum (venturus/venturum/venturos) esse.
2 putamus milites tribus diebus (adventuros/adventuras/adventuram) esse.
3 spero te mox (rediturus/redituram/rediturum) esse.
4 scimus (eam/eos/eum) mox ingressuram esse.
5 putat (omnes/neminem/paucos) discessurum esse.
6 sperasne (eos, eum, eam) secuturos esse?
7 scisne puellas cras (abituras esse/abire/abiisse)?
8 audivi Iudaeos paucis diebus amphitheatrum (conficere/confecturum esse/confecturos esse).
9 respondent servi se heri quam celerrime (currere/cucurrisse/cursuros esse).
10 Eucleides dicit se epistolam cras (conficere/confecisse/confecturum esse).

34

## Exercise 46c

*Using Story 46 as a guide, translate into Latin:*

1 Titus is sure that Cornelius will not work tomorrow.
2 He does not realise that his brother said this in fun.
3 I see that the streets are full of people.
4 It is agreed that Aurelia does not like blood.
5 I hope that we shall see you in the amphitheatre.
6 Titus knows that Cornelius is always busy.

# The Colosseum

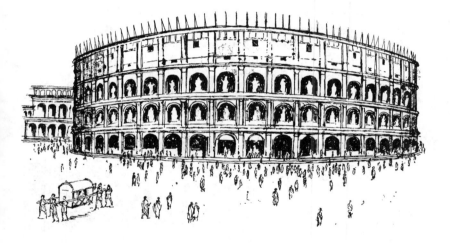

When the family of Cornelius returned to Rome, the great building of the Colosseum was nearing completion. Until this time, Rome's amphitheatres had usually been temporary wooden structures and these caused some frightful disasters, as at Fidenae near Rome in AD 27, when a wooden amphitheatre collapsed, killing or maiming 50000 people. Wooden structures continued to be built even after the completion of the magnificent architectural monument known to its contemporaries as the **Amphitheatrum Flavium** but familiar to us as the Colosseum.

Begun by Vespasian, the Colosseum was dedicated in June AD 80 by his son Titus, who had used Jewish prisoners to speed up its construction. The massive elliptical building rose in four tiers and measured overall 189 × 156 metres. With seating space estimated at 45000, it could be covered over by a massive awning in excessive heat or rain—though Gaius Caligula is said to have taken delight in opening such awnings in times of extreme heat and forbidding anyone to leave! It took 1000 sailors of the Imperial fleet to raise this awning.

Admission was free and open to men, women and children, slave or free, so long as places were available. Women were confined to the topmost area and their view must certainly have been restricted.

The floor of the Colosseum was of timber, strewn with sand, and would contain numerous trapdoors. Under the arena, and extending beyond it, was a vast complex of subterranean cells and passages which now lie open and exposed to view. Remains can be seen of lifts and machinery (worked by counter-weights) used to raise at various points in the arena caged animals, scenery and other apparatus needed for wild beast hunts.

On the occasion of the dedication of the Colosseum, Emperor Titus held a festival for 100 days and during the celebrations staged a very lavish gladiatorial show.

The interior of the Colosseum as it is today. (Photograph, Peter Clayton)

# 47

# A Day at
# the Colosseum

A day at the Colosseum was a great occasion. Tickets (**tesserae**), shown to the gate-keepers (**apparitores**), were numbered according to the seating areas in the Amphitheatre. Seventy-six main entrances and numerous marble plaques illustrating the seating areas enabled the crowd to move swiftly and efficiently through a network of passages, stairs and ramps to their correct place. The officiating magistrate, usually the emperor in Rome, would go to the imperial seat of honour (**pulvinar**), and then the show could begin. The gladiators would parade, and stop before the **pulvinar**: they would greet the emperor with the words: "Hail, Caesar! Those who are about to die give you greetings." (**ave, Caesar! morituri te salutant.**) Next the band (**cornicines** and **tubicines**) would strike up. Then came the games. Pairs (**paria**) of gladiators would fight, urged on by the trainers (**lanistae**). The people joined in with roars of "Thrash him!" (**verbera!**), "Murder him!" (**iugula!**), "He's hit!" (**hoc habet!**), "Let him go!" (**mitte!**). The savagery reached a peak with the midday fighters (**meridiani**), usually condemned criminals.

prope amphitheatrum omnes viae erant plenae hominum qui ad spectaculum veniebant. undique clamor ac strepitus; undique cives, feminae, servi. multi totam noctem extra amphitheatri portas morati erant. nunc adfuit hora spectaculi.

Cornelius, cum tesseras apparitoribus ostendisset, ad locum magistratibus reservatum cum Marco a servo ductus est. Marcus tot et tam varios homines numquam viderat. dum attonitus circumspicit, subito vidit Titum iam consedisse. patruum rogare cupiebat quando pervenisset, nam sciebat Titum sero ex lecto surgere solere. sed, quod pater aderat, Marcus nihil dixit. quam ingens erat amphitheatrum! quanta erat spectatorum turba! Marcus coniciebat quot spectatores amphitheatro contineri possent cum subito fuit silentium.

omnes ad pulvinar oculos converterunt.

"ecce!" clamavit Titus. "iam intrat Caesar, amor ac deliciae generis humani!"

tum, clamore sublato, spectatores principem una voce salutaverunt. stupuit Marcus, admiratione captus. iam gladiatores cuncti contra pulvinar constiterant. "ave, Caesar!" clamaverunt. "morituri te salutant." exierunt gladiatores. mox tubicines et cornicines. postremo gladiatorum paria in arenam intraverunt.

nunc undique erat clamor, tumultus, furor. lanistae huc illuc concursantes "verbera!" "iugula!" clamabant; turba "hoc habet!" aut "mitte!" aut "iugula!" Marcus nihil tale prius viderat. complures horas acriter pugnabatur; haud minus ferociter a spectatoribus clamabatur.

subito Cornelius "nunc" inquit "domum nobis redeundum est. mox enim pugnabunt meridiani, quos alias tu, Marce, videbis."

"nonne tu quoque discedere vis, patrue?" clamavit Marcus.

cui respondit Titus se discedere nolle; se nondum satis vidisse; meridianos mox in arenam venturos esse. brevi tempore Marcus cum Cornelio in lectica per urbem portabatur et secum cogitabat "quid ego primum Sexto narrabo?"

---

**tot,** so many

**coniciebat,** was trying to guess

**contineri,** to be contained (present infinitive passive)

**amor ac deliciae generis humani,** the darling and delight of mankind

**admiratione captus,** in utter amazement

**contra** ( + *acc.*), opposite, in front of

**furor, furoris** (*m*), frenzy

**prius,** previously

**acriter,** fiercely

**pugnabatur,** the fighting went on

**nobis redeundum est,** we must return

**alias,** at another time

---

**ostendo, ostendere** (3), **ostendi, ostentum,** to show, point out
**converto, convertere** (3), **converti, conversum,** to turn (round)
**tollo, tollere** (3), **sustuli, sublatum,** to lift, raise
**consisto, consistere** (3), **constiti,** to halt, stop, stand

# Exercise 47a

*Translate:*

1  Titus respondet se domum redire nolle.
2  nos omnes scimus Marcum ad amphitheatrum ivisse.
3  pro certo habemus Titum sero perventurum esse.

## Accusative and Infinitive III

So far, the verbs of *thinking*, *knowing*, *saying*, *seeing*, etc., have usually been in the present tense. Now look carefully at the following three sentences and compare them with the three sentences in Exercise 47a:

Titus respondit se domum redire nolle.
*Titus replied that he **was** unwilling to return home.*

nos omnes sciebamus Marcum ad amphitheatrum ivisse.
*We all knew that Marcus **had** gone to the amphitheatre.*

pro certo habebamus Titum sero perventurum esse.
*We were sure that Titus **would** arrive late.*

After the past tenses **habebamus**, **respondit** and **sciebamus**, although the accusative and infinitive clauses are exactly the same in Latin as they were in Exercise 47a, in English

the present infinitive is translated by *was unwilling*
the perfect infinitive is translated by *had gone*
the future infinitive is translated by *would arrive*

## Exercise 47b

*Translate:*

1  Titus speravit pueros ad munera ituros esse.
2  Marcus dixit patrem epistolam confecisse.
3  audivi Cornelium ad Curiam festinare.
4  Cornelius dixit se Marcum secum ducturum esse.
5  num credidisti Corneliam pupa ludere?
6  pro certo habebam Aureliam nobiscum non ituram esse.
7  Aurelia sciebat Corneliam pupam filiae Davi dedisse.
8  patruus meus respondit se manere malle.

## Exercise 47c

*Translate:*

1. Cornelius putavit Titum discedere.
2. Marcus vidit Titum iam adesse.
3. Sextus dixit Marcum domum mature rediturum esse.
4. Cornelius scit Marcum principem non vidisse.
5. Marcus videt cives omnes esse laetos.
6. Titus dixit gladiatores in amphitheatro pugnaturos esse.
7. Marcus putavit se numquam tot et tam varios homines vidisse.
8. pater dicit gladiatores amphitheatrum mox intraturos esse.
9. putabat se tantos clamores numquam audivisse.
10. Titus dicit meridianos nondum in arenam venisse.

## People at Work

Many words in Latin show by their form the kind of meaning they have. For example, nouns that end in **-tor** or **-sor** indicate "a person-who-does something", e.g.

> **emptor** (person who buys—**emere**), *a buyer*

This type of word is often formed from the supine of a verb. What would the following people do?

> spectator, amator, laudator, orator, pugnator, cantor, dictator, doctor, imperator, defensor, victor, captor, navigator, successor, sponsor.

Some are formed from nouns that indicate their sphere of activity:

> ianitor, viator, gladiator.

What do the following mean?

> victor ludorum
> fidei defensor
> doctor litterarum
> Iesus Hominum Salvator (IHS)
> laudator temporis acti

# Gladiators

Criminals sentenced to death could be purchased cheaply and thrown to the beasts or made to fight to the death unarmed in the arena. But those convicted of lesser crimes, for which the mines or deportation was the penalty, might instead go to a gladiatorial school. Slaves acquired through war or piracy were another source of recruitment, and occasionally volunteers, including Roman citizens, actually took up the gladiatorial trade. All gladiators bound themselves to their trade by an oath which laid down the severest penalties for backsliders or runaways: "to be burnt with fire, shackled with chains, beaten with rods and killed with steel" (**uri, vinciri, verberari, ferroque necari.**)

After thorough training in the barracks, the gladiator was ready for the arena. Successful gladiators, like chariot drivers, were popular heroes. This is an inscription from Pompeii:

> Celadios the Thracian, three fights, three victories, the answer to a maiden's prayer.

Victorious gladiators were richly rewarded and, after a period of service, might win the wooden sword of freedom, even if slaves. Veteran gladiators could also be employed as overseers in the gladiatorial schools.

The fate of a defeated gladiator rested with the mob. If he had won favour, the mob might wave their handkerchiefs and the emperor or presiding magistrate might then signal for his release. Otherwise the thumbs-down sign indicated that the fallen gladiator should speedily be killed.

There were various classes of gladiator—these included the heavily armed Samnite with oblong shield, visored helmet and short sword; the Thracian carrying a small round shield and curved scimitar; the **mirmillo**, or "fish man", who wore a helmet with a fish emblem on it and was armed with a sword and large shield; and the **retiarius**, or "net man", who was unarmed but for a great net and sharp trident. Each had his own supporters: the Emperor Titus, for example, supported the Thracians, as did Caligula. Local rivalry, too, was common as is borne out by this inscription from Pompeii:

> Luck to the people of Puteoli and all those from Nuceria; down with the Pompeians.

Such rivalry could lead to trouble, as this incident in the reign of Nero illustrates:

About this time there was a serious riot involving the people of Pompeii and Nuceria. It started with a small incident at a gladiatorial show. Insults were being exchanged, as often happens in these disorderly country towns. Abuse changed to stone-throwing, and then swords were drawn. The games were held in Pompeii and the locals came off best. Many badly wounded Nucerians were taken to their city. Many parents and children were bereaved. The emperor ordered the Senate to inquire into the matter and the Senate passed it on to the consuls. As a result of their report, the Senate banned Pompeii from holding any similar event for ten years.

Tacitus, *Annals XIV. 16*

**non te peto, piscem peto, quid me fugis, Galle?** *It is not you I am aiming at, but the fish. Why do you flee from me, Gallus?*

# Exercise 47d (Revision)

## Marcus reports back

Marcus iam domum regressus omnia quae viderat Sexto narrabat:

"cum amphitheatro appropinquaremus, vidimus magnam hominum multitudinem per portas intrare. nos ipsi ingressi vidimus multa milia civium iam consedisse. ego non credidissem tot homines amphitheatro contineri posse. patruum exspectare volui, sed pater mihi dixit Titum sine dubio iam adesse. et recte dixit; nam, cum ad locum magistratibus reservatum venissemus, vidimus Titum eo iam ductum esse.

subito undique clamatum est. deinde vidi principem a gladiatoribus salutari. quam fortiter incedebant hi gladiatores! multi tamen eorum morituri erant. ubi pugnam commiserunt, spectabam obstupefactus. nihil tale prius videram. vidi multos vulnerari atque complures quidem occidi. quam fortes erant gladiatores!

maxime dolebam quod ante meridiem domum nobis redeundum erat. Titus dixit se malle manere, cum cuperet meridianos videre. spero patrem me ad amphitheatrum iterum ducturum esse. fortasse te quoque ducet."

**credidissem,** I would
  have believed
**clamatum est,** there
  was shouting
**pugnam committere,**
  to join battle
**obstupefactus, -a, -um,**
  astounded

**salutari***  ⎫
**vulnerari*** ⎬ see note
**occidi***    ⎭ below

**incedo, incedere** (3), **incessi, incessum,** to march

\* **vidi principem salutari,** I saw that the emperor was being hailed. The form **salutari** is present infinitive passive. The other present infinitives passive (**vulnerari** and **occidi**) should be treated in the same way.

# Accusative and Infinitive IV

Passive infinitives also are used in this construction:

1 vidi multos **vulnerari** atque complures quidem **occidi**.
*I saw that many* **were being wounded** *and several actually* **were being killed**.

The present infinitive passive can be recognised by the ending **-ri** in Groups 1, 2 and 4 and by the ending **-i** in Group 3.

2 vidimus Titum eo iam **ductum esse**.
*We saw that Titus* **had** *already* **been taken** *there*.

The perfect infinitive passive is formed from the participle **ductus, -a, -um** and **esse**.

## Exercise 47e

*Translate:*
1 Eucleides vidit Corneliam a pueris vexari.
2 Sextus nescivit vocem suam auditam esse.
3 vidimus complures naves iam deletas esse.
4 putaverunt vestimenta a servo custodiri.
5 scivi milites in Britanniam mitti.
6 fures sciverunt se in apodyterio conspectos esse.

## VERBS: Infinitives

You have now met the following forms of the infinitive:

*Present*

| | Active | Passive |
|---|---|---|
| 1 | **portare,** to carry | **portari,** to be carried |
| 2 | **movere,** to move | **moveri,** to be moved |
| 3 | **mittere,** to send | **mitti,** to be sent |
| 4 | **audire,** to hear | **audiri,** to be heard |

*Perfect*

|   | Active | Passive |
|---|--------|---------|
| 1 | **portavisse,**<br>to have carried | **portatus, -a, -um esse,**<br>to have been carried |
| 2 | **movisse,**<br>to have moved | **motus, -a, -um esse,**<br>to have been moved |
| 3 | **misisse,**<br>to have sent | **missus, -a, -um esse,**<br>to have been sent |
| 4 | **audivisse,**<br>to have heard | **auditus, -a, -um esse,**<br>to have been heard |

*Future*

|   | Active |
|---|--------|
| 1 | **portaturus, -a, -um esse,** to be about to carry |
| 2 | **moturus, -a, -um esse,** to be about to move |
| 3 | **missurus, -a, -um esse,** to be about to send |
| 4 | **auditurus, -a, -um esse,** to be about to hear |

N.B. The future infinitive passive rarely appears in Latin.

## Deponent Verbs:

The present and perfect infinitives of deponent verbs are passive in form; the future infinitive is active in form. All three tenses are active in meaning. For example,

| *Present* | *Perfect* | *Future* |
|-----------|-----------|----------|
| **conari,**<br>to try | **conatus, -a, -um esse,**<br>to have tried | **conaturus, -a, -um esse,**<br>to be about to try |
| **sequi,**<br>to follow | **secutus, -a, -um esse,**<br>to have followed | **secuturus, -a, -um esse,**<br>to be about to follow |

45

# Other Shows in the Arena

The Emperor Titus also held a sea-fight (**naumachia**) on the old artificial lake of Augustus and afterwards used the empty basin of the lake for still more gladiatorial bouts and a wild-beast hunt (**venatio**) in which over 5000 animals of different kinds died in a single day. His brother and imperial successor, Domitian, was not to be outdone; he even used the Colosseum itself as a lake! In his life of Domitian Suetonius writes:

> Domitian constantly gave lavish entertainments both in the Amphitheatre and in the Circus. As well as the usual races with two-horse and four-horse chariots, he put on two battles, one with infantry and one with cavalry; he also exhibited a naval battle in his amphitheatre. He gave hunts of wild beasts and gladiatorial fights at night by torchlight, and even fights between women.
>
> He staged sea battles with almost full-sized fleets. For these he had a pool dug near the Tiber and seats built round it. He even went on watching these events in torrential rain.
>
> Suetonius, *Domitian 4*

Gladiators were not used to fight animals (**bestiae**) in the wild-beast hunts. For this, special fighters, **bestiarii**, were employed. In these shows, such animals as lions, tigers, bears, bulls, hippopotami, elephants, crocodiles, deer, pigs and even ostriches were made to fight each other or the **bestiarii**, or else driven to attack condemned criminals, who were sometimes chained or nailed to stakes. When Trajan held four months of festivities to celebrate his Dacian wars, some 10000 gladiators and over 11000 animals appeared in the arena over this period.

Even before the time of the emperors we read of the provinces being scoured for animals for these shows. Caelius in a letter to his friend Cicero wrote:

> Curio is very generous to me and has put me under an obligation; for if he had not given me the animals which had been shipped from Africa for his own games, I would not have been able to continue with mine. But, as I must go on, I should be glad if you would do your best to let me have some animals from your province—I am continually making this request.
>
> Cicero, *Epistolae ad Familiares VIII. 8*

Venatio

## Word Families

In Latin whole families of words are sometimes built from a
single root:

**liber,** free

**liberare,** to free

**libertas,** freedom

**liberator,** person who sets
free

**libertus,** freedman

**liberalis,** free, generous

**liberaliter,** freely,
generously

**amor,** love

**amare,** to love

**amator,** lover

**amabilis,** lovable

**amicitia,** friendship

**amica,** friend

**amicus,** friend

**inimicus,** enemy

# 48
# Androcles
# and the Lion

olim in Circo Maximo ludus bestiarius populo dabatur. omnes spectatoribus admirationi fuerunt leones, sed unus ex eis videbatur saevissimus. ad pugnam bestiariam introductus erat inter complures servus quidam cui Androcles nomen fuit. quem cum ille leo procul vidisset, subito quasi admirans stetit ac deinde lente et placide homini appropinquabat. tum caudam clementer et blande movens, manus hominis, prope iam metu exanimati, lingua lambit. Androcles, animo iam recuperato, leonem attentius spectavit. tum, quasi mutua recognitione facta, laeti ibi stabant et homo et leo.

ea res tam mirabilis turbam maxime excitavit. Androclem ad pulvinar arcessitum rogavit Caesar cur ille saevissimus leo ei soli pepercisset. tum Androcles rem mirabilem narravit.

"dum ego in Africa cum domino meo habito," inquit "propter eius crudelitatem fugere coactus in speluncam confugi. haud multo post ad eandem speluncam venit hic leo gemens et dolens, uno pede claudus. atque primo quidem terroris plenus latebam. sed leo, cum me conspexisset, mitis et mansuetus appropinquavit atque pedem mihi ostendit, quasi auxilium petens. stirpem ingentem, quae in eius pede haerebat, ego extraxi ac iam sine magno timore vulnus lavi. tum ille, pede in manibus meis posito, recubuit et dormivit. tres annos ego et leo in eadem spelunca habitabamus, eodem cibo vescentes. postea captus a militibus, reductus sum ad dominum qui me statim ad bestias condemnavit."

princeps, fabula servi audita, maxime admirabatur. Androcles omnium consensu liberatus est, datusque ei leo.

**admirationi esse,** to be
a source of wonder or
surprise (to)

**quasi,** as if
**placide,** quietly, tamely

**clementer et blande,** in
a gentle, friendly way
**metu exanimatus,**
paralysed with fear
**mutua recognitione
facta,** recognising one
another
**crudelitas,
crudelitatis** (*f*),
cruelty

**claudus, -a, -um,** lame
**lateo** (2), to lie in hiding, hide
**mitis, mitis, mite,** gentle
**mansuetus, -a, -um,**
tame
**stirps, stirpis** (*f*),
thorn
**omnium consensu,** by
general agreement

**admiror, admirari** (1), **admiratus sum,** to wonder (at)
**lambo, lambere** (3), **lambi,** to lick
**parco, parcere** (3), **peperci, parsum** ( + *dat.*), to spare
**cogo, cogere** (3), **coegi, coactum,** to compel, force
**confugio, confugere** (3), **confugi,** to flee for refuge
**vescor, vesci** (3) ( + *abl.*), to feed (on)

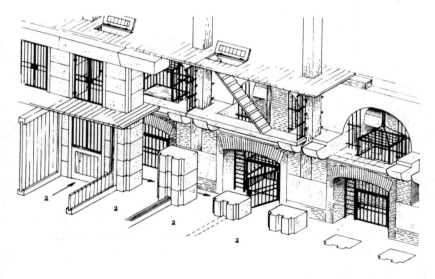

This diagram shows the cages for wild animals under the floor of the Colosseum.
The animals were brought in through an entry (marked a). The cages were hoisted
to a higher floor directly below the arena and from there the animals were driven up
a gangway and into the arena through a hatch.

49

# Building up the Meaning of a Sentence IV

*Look at the following sentences:*
    audivit cur pater advenisset.
    *He heard why father had arrived.*

    clamores servorum audivit.
    *He heard the shouts of the slaves.*

    audivit patrem ad urbem advenisse.
    *He heard that father had reached the city.*

You will see that the sense after *heard* can develop in three different ways:

    He heard who, what, how, etc.      *question*
    He heard someone/something         *accusative*
    He heard that. . . .               *accusative and infinitive*

When you meet **audio** you must expect one of these three possibilities:

1 **audio cur, quis, quid, quando, quot,** etc. (Translate straight on.)
    e.g. audio quid dicas.
        *I hear what you are saying.*

2 **audio** *accusative:*
    e.g. audio servos. . . . (Wait to see if there is also an *infinitive*.)
    (*a*) If there is no infinitive, the accusative is the object of **audio,**
    e.g. audio servos     in viis clamantes.
        *I hear the slaves     shouting in the streets.*
    (*b*) If there is, insert *that* . . . and continue with the translation of the accusative,
    e.g. audio           servos cenam paravisse.
        *I hear (that)     the slaves have prepared dinner.*

The following verbs have to be treated in the same way:

    **scio,** I know              **intellego,** I understand
    **video,** I see              **sentio,** I realise

## Exercise 48a

*Translate:*

1. pueri audiverunt gladiatores principem salutantes.
2. Eucleides non sensit ubi essent pueri.
3. Marcus vidit gladiatores iam in arenam intravisse.
4. spectatores non intellegunt cur leo manus servi lambat.
5. Cornelius sciebat locum magistratibus reservatum esse.
6. Androcles dixit se stirpem e pede leonis extraxisse.
7. Pyramus credebat Thisben a leone occisam esse.
8. nonne audis illos leones strepitum maximum facientes?
9. ita vero! leones audio; sed cives maiorem strepitum facere videntur.
10. cives intellegebant servos saepe fugere cogi.

## Exercise 48b

*Translate:*

1. puer nesciebat quot gladiatores vulnerati essent.
2. Androcles dixit leonem uno pede claudum ad speluncam venisse.
3. scivistine bestias sub arena contineri? ipse eas audivi.
4. cives pro certo habebant nullos gladiatores effugere conaturos esse.
5. cives audire cupiebant cur leo hominem non necavisset.
6. fur nesciebat se a Sexto conspici.
7. spectatores viderunt leonem caudam clementer moventem.
8. spectatores viderunt unum leonem saevissimum esse.
9. Marcus audivit patrem e domo egredientem.
10. Androcles non intellexit cur leo pedem sibi ostenderet.

A gladiator's helmet embossed with figures representing Rome and its provinces. (Photograph, The Mansell Collection)

# 49
# Audience Reaction

## SCENE I: In the Amphitheatre

(*Licinius Caeliusque, duo spectatores in amphitheatro sedentes, inter se loquuntur.*)

LICINIUS: ecce! in arenam veniunt gladiatores! scisne quot sint?

CAELIUS: minime vero! scisne tu quot leones, quot tigres adsint? ego audivi multos leones ingentes ab Africa allatos esse et sub arena in caveis teneri.

(*intrat Postumius qui sero venire solet.*)

POSTUMIUS: video principem iam advenisse et a civibus salutari.

CAELIUS: ecce! iam gladiatores eum salutant! eheu! sciunt se morituros esse.

POSTUMIUS: tacete! audio bestias! videtisne leones in arenam immitti?

LICINIUS: ecce bestia immanis! servo illi parvo numquam parcet! iam pugnare incipiunt. euge!

POSTUMIUS: euge! ... at constitit leo! miror cur leo constiterit!

CAELIUS: num credis eum re vera constitisse? pro certo habeo eum mox impetum ferociter facturum esse.

LICINIUS: at video leonem lente et placide homini appropinquantem. mehercule! videsne eum manus hominis lingua lambentem? scio leonem esse saevissimum. nescio cur hominem non occidat.

CAELIUS: videsne servum leonem spectantem? timere non videtur.

POSTUMIUS: video servum a principe arcessitum esse. miror quid dicat.

## SCENE II: Leaving the Amphitheatre

LICINIUS: non poteram intellegere cur leo impetum non fecisset. mirum quidem erat spectaculum.

| | |
|---|---|
| CAELIUS: | audivi leonem a principe homini datum esse. |
| POSTUMIUS: | ita vero! sed ecce! Paetus venit. salve, Paete! |
| PAETUS: | cur hunc tantum clamorem facitis? |
| CAELIUS: | hoc vix credes! vidimus leonem, bestiam saevissimam, servi manus lambentem! nescimus cur manus non devoraverit. |
| PAETUS: | quid? nonne audivistis causam? leo ille sensit se hominem antea vidisse. homo principi narravit quomodo stirpem olim e pede leonis extraxisset. narravit se et leonem in Africa in eadem spelunca tres annos habitavisse. ubi captus est, putavit se numquam iterum leonem visurum esse. nesciebat quo leo ivisset. |
| POSTUMIUS: | agite! sero est. esurio! domum redeamus. fortasse videbimus servum leonem per vias ducentem. |

**cavea, -ae** (*f*), cage
**immanis, -is, -e,** huge
**re vera,** really

**impetus, -us** (*m*), attack
**redeamus,** let us return

**immitto, immittere, immisi, immissum,** to send in, release
**incipio, incipere** (3), **incepi, inceptum,** to begin
**miror, mirari** (1), **miratus sum,** to wonder
**intellego, intellegere** (3), **intellexi, intellectum,** to understand,
    realise

# Gladiatorial Fever

Sometimes high-born Romans were so enthusiastic about the combats in the arena that they took part themselves as gladiators. The Roman poet Juvenal, and Romans generally, strongly disapproved:

There in the arena you have a disgrace to the city: Gracchus fighting not in the arms of a **mirmillo** with shield and sabre, for

53

he scorns and rejects such equipment; nor does he hide his face with a visor. Look! it's a trident he sports; he shakes his trailing net in his right hand, casts and misses. Then he holds up his naked face for all to see and runs frantically around the whole arena, easily recognisable!

Juvenal, Satires VIII. 199–206

## Opposition to the Games

Some Romans protested at the brutality of these shows. Seneca writes about the midday "interval" between the morning and afternoon sessions. In this interval criminals were forced to fight in the arena until everyone was dead:

> Nothing is so harmful to good character as attending the games. I happened to attend a midday performance expecting some sport, fun and relaxation where men's eyes would get a rest from the sight of human blood. It was the very opposite. There had been compassion in the previous fights but now they stop playing and this is sheer murder. The men have no armour. They are completely exposed to all blows and every blow draws blood. Many prefer this exhibition to the ordinary pairs and challenge matches. Of course they do. There is no helmet or shield to deflect the weapon. What's the use of skill or armour? They simply delay the killing. In the morning, men are thrown to lions and bears— at noon to the spectators. The killer in one bout next faces the man who will kill him. The last winner is kept for another day's slaughter.

Seneca, Epistolae Morales 7

After Seneca, others came out against the institution of the games. Among these were Christian writers like Tertullian and Augustine. The Emperor Constantine made a decree of abolition but this seems not to have been enforced. Gladiatorial shows were finally suppressed by Honorius (Emperor of the West AD 395–423) though other blood-sports in the arena continued for several centuries after this.

# 50
# Nothing Ever Happens

sol caelo sereno lucebat. cantabant aves. natura ipsa gaudere videbatur. tristi vultu tamen sedebat Cornelia sola in peristylio. secum cogitabat: "me taedet solitudinis. cur nemo me observat? cur mecum nemo loquitur? pater tantum temporis in tablino agit ut eum numquam videam. mater tam occupata est ut mecum numquam loquatur. Marcus et Sextus suis ludis adeo dediti sunt ut nihil aliud faciant. non intellego cur nuper etiam servae me neglexerint, cur Eucleides ille verbosus verbum nullum mihi dixerit. o me miseram!"

Corneliae haec cogitanti "heus tu, Cornelia!" clamavit Marcus qui tum intravit in peristylium. "pater iubet te in tablino statim adesse. festinare te oportet."

Cornelia, cum in tablinum intravisset, vidit adesse et patrem et matrem, id quod erat ei admirationi et curae.

tum pater gravi vultu "olim, Cornelia," inquit "Publius Cornelius Scipio Africanus, vir praeclarissimus gentis nostrae, dicitur inter epulas senatorum filiam suam Tiberio Graccho despondisse. post epulas, cum Scipio domum regressus uxori dixisset se filiam despondisse, illa maxima ira est commota. 'non decet patrem' inquit 'despondere filiam, inscia matre.' at pater tuus non est Publio Cornelio similis, nam una constituimus et ego et mater tua iuveni cuidam nobili te despondere. Quintus Valerius, adulescens ille optimus, vult te in matrimonium ducere, id quod nobis placet. placetne tibi, Cornelia?"

Cornelia adeo perturbata est ut vix loqui posset, sed tandem submissa voce "mihi quoque placet" respondit.

cui Cornelius "cras aderit Valerius ipse."

**sol, solis** (*m*), sun
**serenus, -a, -um,** clear, bright
**avis, avis** (*m/f*), bird

**me taedet** ( + *gen.*), I am tired (of)
**observo** ( 1 ), to pay attention to

55

**adeo,** so much, to such an extent

**deditus, -a, -um,** devoted, dedicated

**nuper,** recently

**te oportet** ( + *infinitive*), you must

**id quod,** (a thing) which

**curae esse,** to be a cause of anxiety (to)

**gens, gentis** ( *f* ), family, clan

**epulae, -arum** ( *f.pl* ), banquet, feast

**non decet patrem,** a father should not

**similis, -is, -e** ( + *dat.* ), like, similar (to)

**iuvenis, -is** ( *m* ), young man

**submissa voce,** in a subdued voice

**neglego, neglegere** (3), **neglexi, neglectum,** to neglect, ignore
**despondeo, despondere** (2), **despondi, desponsum,** to betroth, promise in marriage

# RESULT CLAUSES

When you meet these words

**tam,** so
**tot,** so many
**adeo,** so, to such a degree
**ita,** in such a way

**tantus,** so great
**tantum,** so much
**talis,** such

you will often find the word **ut** later in the sentence meaning *that,* followed by a clause indicating result,
e.g. **adeo** perturbata est **ut** vix loqui posset.
*She was **so** embarrassed **that** she could hardly speak.*

**tam** occupata est **ut** mecum numquam loquatur.
*She is **so** busy **that** she never speaks to me.*

The verb in the result clause is in the subjunctive and is translated into the equivalent tense of the indicative.

# VERBS: Subjunctive Mood

The imperfect and pluperfect subjunctives were tabulated on page 8. The following is the tabulation of the present and perfect subjunctives:

## Present Tense
*Active:*

| Group 1 | Group 2 | Group 3 | Group 4 |
|---------|---------|---------|---------|
| portem | moveam | mittam | audiam |
| portes | moveas | mittas | audias |
| portet | moveat | mittat | audiat |
| portemus | moveamus | mittamus | audiamus |
| portetis | moveatis | mittatis | audiatis |
| portent | moveant | mittant | audiant |

*Passive:*

| | | | |
|---------|---------|---------|---------|
| porter | movear | mittar | audiar |
| porteris | movearis | mittaris | audiaris |
| portetur | moveatur | mittatur | audiatur |
| portemur | moveamur | mittamur | audiamur |
| portemini | moveamini | mittamini | audiamini |
| portentur | moveantur | mittantur | audiantur |

## Perfect Tense
*Active:*

| | | | |
|---------|---------|---------|---------|
| portaverim | moverim | miserim | audiverim |
| portaveris | moveris | miseris | audiveris |
| portaverit | moverit | miserit | audiverit |
| portaverimus | moverimus | miserimus | audiverimus |
| portaveritis | moveritis | miseritis | audiveritis |
| portaverint | moverint | miserint | audiverint |

*Passive:*

| | | | |
|---------|---------|---------|---------|
| portatus sim | motus sim | missus sim | auditus sim |
| portatus sis | motus sis | missus sis | auditus sis |
| etc. | etc. | etc. | etc. |

# IRREGULAR VERBS: Subjunctive Mood

## Present:

| | | | | | |
|---|---|---|---|---|---|
| sim | possim | velim | nolim | malim | eam |
| sis | possis | velis | nolis | malis | eas |
| sit | possit | velit | nolit | malit | eat |
| simus | possimus | velimus | nolimus | malimus | eamus |
| sitis | possitis | velitis | nolitis | malitis | eatis |
| sint | possint | velint | nolint | malint | eant |

## Perfect:

| | | | | | |
|---|---|---|---|---|---|
| fuerim | potuerim | voluerim | noluerim | maluerim | iverim |
| fueris | potueris | volueris | nolueris | malueris | iveris |
| fuerit | potuerit | voluerit | noluerit | maluerit | iverit |
| fuerimus | potuerimus | voluerimus | noluerimus | maluerimus | iverimus |
| fueritis | potueritis | volueritis | nolueritis | malueritis | iveritis |
| fuerint | potuerint | voluerint | noluerint | maluerint | iverint |

# Exercise 50a

*Translate:*

1 tam laete cantabant aves ut natura ipsa gaudere videretur.
2 leo tantus et tam ferox erat ut servus metu exanimatus ceciderit.
3 tot spectatores ad ludos convenerant ut Circus vix omnes contineret.
4 Cornelii filia adeo perturbata est ut submissa voce responderet.
5 tanta tempestas coorta erat ut sero Brundisium advenerimus.
6 Cornelia non rogavit cur pater se Valerio despondisset.
7 talis iuvenis erat Valerius ut Cornelio placeret filiam ei despondere.
8 Cornelia tam laeta subito facta est ut omnia Flaviae narrare cuperet.
9 Cornelia "tam laeta sum" inquit "ut vix loqui possim."
10 pater tam gravi vultu locutus est ut Cornelia miraretur quid accidisset.

# Roman Weddings I

When a Roman girl reached marriageable age—somewhere between twelve and fourteen—her father set about finding her a husband.

When a friend asked the writer Pliny to help him find a suitable match for his niece, Pliny wrote back to say that a certain Acilianus would be just the man. After speaking highly of Acilianus' father, his grandmother on his mother's side and his uncle, he describes the prospective bridegroom as follows:

> Acilianus himself is a person of very great energy and application, but at the same time exceedingly modest. He has held the offices of quaestor, tribune and praetor with very great distinction and this relieves you of the need to canvass on his behalf. His expression is frank and open; his complexion is fresh and he has a healthy colour; his whole bearing is noble and handsome with the dignity of a senator. I don't know whether I should add that his father has ample means; for, when I picture you and your brother for whom we are seeking a son-in-law, I think there is no need for me to say more on that subject; and yet, when I consider the attitudes of people nowadays and even the laws of the country, which judge a man's income as of primary importance, I'm probably right in thinking that even a reference to his father's means should not be omitted. Certainly, if one thinks of the children of the marriage and their children, one must take the question of money into account when making a choice.

Pliny, *Epistles I. 14*

When we remember that a Roman would be nearly forty before he attained the praetorship, Pliny's candidate (if we read between the lines) was probably red-faced, stout and middle-aged, but Pliny seems to consider these points less important than having good family connections and plenty of money.

So our thirteen-year-old Cornelia might find herself engaged to a mere boy (minimum age fourteen) or to someone three times her age, but she was not expected to raise any objections to what was simply a legal contract between families.

Before the actual wedding, a betrothal ceremony (**sponsalia**) often took place, witnessed by relatives and friends. The father of the girl was asked formally if he "promised" his daughter and replied that he did. (Question: **spondesne?** Answer: **spondeo.**) Gifts were then given to the bride-to-be, including a ring (**anulus**) either of gold or of iron set in gold. This was worn on the third finger of the left hand, from which it was believed a nerve ran straight to the heart.

Usually, the two families had already discussed the terms of the dowry (**dos, dotis**), which was returnable in the event of a divorce.

A betrothal ring.
(Reproduced by courtesy of the Trustees of the British Museum)

## Exercise 50b

omnia iam diu ad sponsalia parata erant, inscia Cornelia. Valerius enim, cum primum Brundisium e nave egressus est, ad Cornelium scripserat se velle Corneliam in matrimonium ducere; deinde Cornelius rescripserat se libenter filiam Valerio desponsurum esse; tum Aurelia Viniam, matrem Flaviae, invitaverat ut pronuba esset. ad sponsalia igitur Valerius et Vinia et Flavia Romam iam advenerant.

aderat dies sponsalium. quinta hora omnes Cornelii atque propinqui amicique in atrium convenerunt. deinde, silentio facto, Cornelia vultu demisso ingressa in atrium deducta est. tum Valerius, qui contra Cornelium in medio atrio stabat, ei "spondesne" ait "te filiam tuam mihi uxorem daturum esse?"

cui Cornelius "spondeo."

quo dicto, Valerius ad Corneliam conversus anulum aureum tertio digito sinistrae manus eius aptavit. tum osculum ei dedit. omnes sponso et sponsae gratulati sunt.

| | |
|---|---|
| **ad sponsalia,** for the betrothal | **ait,** (he, she) says, said |
| **pronuba, -ae** (*f*), bride's attendant | **conversus, -a, -um,** having turned, turning |
| **propinquus, -i** (*m*), relative | **anulus, -i** (*m*), ring |
| **vultu demisso,** with eyes lowered | **apto** (1), to place, fit |

**spondeo, spondere** (2), **spopondi, sponsum,** to promise solemnly, pledge

**gratulor, gratulari** (1), **gratulatus sum** (+ *dat.*), to congratulate

# 51
# Marcus Comes of Age

Coming of age was an important occasion for a Roman boy and it was marked both by an official ceremony (**officium togae virilis**) and by family celebrations. The ceremony usually took place when the boy had reached the age of sixteen but not on his birthday. It was common for it to be celebrated at the festival called the **Liberalia** in March. It began with the boy dedicating (**consecrare**) the lucky charm (**bulla**) which he had worn since he was a baby and the toga with the purple edge (**toga praetexta**) which boys wore. These he placed before the shrine of the household gods (**lararium**) which was usually in the atrium of the house. From this time on he wore the plain white toga (**toga virilis** or **toga pura**) indicating that he was no longer a boy but a man. After the ceremony members of his family and friends escorted him to the forum (**in forum deducere**). There, in the building where the records were housed (**Tabularium**), his name was entered in the records (**tabulae**). The official ceremony was now completed and the family entertained their friends at a private celebration.

iam aderat mensis Martius. erat dies Liberalium quo die adulescentes Romani togam puram sumere solebant. abhinc complures menses Marcus sedecim annos compleverat; nunc togam virilem sumpturus erat. itaque Cornelius amicos clientesque omnes invitaverat ut eo die in domum convenirent. omnes sciebant patrem Marci divitissimum esse; omnes pro certo habebant eum optimam cenam amicis daturum esse.

domus Gai Cornelii plena erat tumultus, strepitus, clamoris. tot et tam varii homines eo conveniebant ut ianitor, ab ianua progressus, in ipso limine sollicitus staret. si quis appropinquabat, eum magna voce rogabat quis esset et quid vellet. alios rogabat ut in domum procederent, aliis praecipiebat ut in via manerent. nonnulli autem, qui neque amici Cornelii erant neque clientes, ad domum convenerunt, quod sperabant Cornelium se ad cenam invitaturum esse. hi ianitorem orabant ne

se dimitteret; ille autem eis imperabat ut statim discederent.

tandem, omnibus rebus paratis, Cornelius totam familiam rogavit ut in atrium convenirent. aderant propinqui; aderant multi amici; aderant plurimi clientium; aderant omnes servi libertique Corneliorum. cuncti inter se colloquebantur, cuncti gaudebant quod ad hoc officium togae virilis invitati erant.

in atrio ante lararium stabat Marcus togam praetextam bullamque auream in manibus tenens. sensit oculos omnium in se conversos esse. conticuerunt omnes. Marcus primum togam praetextam atque bullam ante lararium depositas Laribus familiaribus consecravit. "nunc" inquit "has res pueriles hic depono. nunc vobis, o Lares familiares, haec libenter consecro."

quo facto, pater servo cuidam imperavit ut togam puram Marco indueret. deinde parentes eum amplexi sunt et ceteri ei gratulati sunt. nunc Marcus, magna comitante caterva, in Forum a patre est deductus.

quo cum pervenissent, Marco ad Tabularium ducto, pater eos qui comitabantur rogavit ut extra Tabularium manerent. ipse una cum filio et paucis propinquis in Tabularium ingressus est, nam ibi nomen Marci in tabulis publicis erat inscribendum.

quibus rebus confectis, omnes adstantes Marcum iam egressum magno clamore salutaverunt. deinde cum Marcus omnibus gratias egisset propter tantam erga se benevolentiam, omnes ad domum Corneliorum redierunt, nam Cornelius multos invitaverat ut apud se eo die cenarent.

**sumere,** to assume (i.e. put on for the first time)
**invitaverat ut,** he had invited (them) to
**ianitor, -oris** (*m*), doorkeeper
**limen, liminis** (*n*), doorstep, doorway
**si quis,** if anyone
**nonnulli, -ae, -a,** some
**oro** (1), to beg
**ne se dimitteret,** not to send them away

**libertus, -i** (*m*), freedman
**Lares, Larum** (*m.pl*), household gods
**familiaris, -is, -e,** belonging to the family
**caterva, -ae** (*f*), crowd
**erat inscribendum,** had to be registered
**gratias agere** ( + *dat.*), to thank
**erga** ( + *acc.*), towards
**benevolentia, -ae** (*f*), kindness

**praecipio, praecipere** (3), **praecepi, praeceptum** ( + *dat.*), to instruct
**impero** (1) ( + *dat.*), to order
**conticesco, conticescere** (3), **conticui,** to fall silent
**amplector, amplecti** (3), **amplexus sum,** to embrace
**comitor, comitari** (1), **comitatus sum,** to accompany

# Telling to, Asking to

Look at these two sentences from the story:

    (a)  alios rogabat **ut** in domum **procederent.**
         *He asked some **to go on** into the house.*
    (b)  hi ianitorem orabant **ne** se **dimitteret.**
         *They kept begging the doorkeeper **not to send** them **away.***

In these sentences **ut** is translated by *to*
                     **ne** is translated by *not to.*

You have already seen **rogo** (I ask), **praecipio** (I instruct), **impero** (I order), **invito** (I invite) and **oro** (I beg) used in this way.

Other verbs are also used like this with **ut** and **ne** followed by the subjunctive:

    **moneo** (I advise, warn); **persuadeo** (I persuade); **hortor** (I urge); **obsecro** (I beg, beseech).

Note the difference between:

    (i)  coquo imperavit ut in atrium veniret.
        *He ordered the cook to come into the atrium.*
    (ii)  imperavit ut coquus arcesseretur.
        *He ordered the cook to be sent for.*

In (i) the order is issued to the cook personally; in (ii) the orders are issued to someone else (not specified). In this latter type of command, "that" is often used, e.g. "He ordered that the cook be sent for."

A sestertius of the Emperor Titus, with the Colosseum on the reverse.
(Reproduced by courtesy of the Trustees of the British Museum)

# Exercise 51a

*Translate:*

1 Cornelius convivas omnes invitavit ut in atrium procederent.
2 tum Cornelius Marco imperavit ut res pueriles Laribus consecraret.
3 Cornelius Marcum toga pura indutum rogavit ut ad forum secum proficisceretur.
4 in Tabulario pater rogavit ut nomen Marci in tabulis publicis inscriberetur.
5 Cornelius omnes convivas invitavit ut apud se cenarent.
6 te oro atque obsecro ut domum venias.
7 noli me hortari ut ad illam urbem eam.
8 te semper moneo ne in media via ambules.
9 Valerius Cornelio persuasit ut Corneliam sibi sponderet.
10 tot homines ad domum Cornelii pervenerunt ut multi intrare non possent.

# Exercise 51b

*Translate:*

1 ianitor iam ianuam claudebat: tam defessus erat ut dormire cuperet.
2 Asellus ianitorem visum rogavit quid eo die fecisset.
3 "tibi dicam" inquit ianitor. "plurimos homines aut ad ianuam accepi aut dimisi."
4 primo omnes hortatus sum ut in via manerent.
5 deinde amicos propinquosque Cornelii rogavi ut intrarent.
6 clientibus praecepi ne statim in domum procederent.
7 nonnulli, quos non prius videram, me oraverunt ne se dimitterem.
8 eos monui ne ad ianuam morarentur.
9 "noli ibi morari" inquam, "nam dominus imperavit ut ianua claudatur."
10 tandem coactus sum servos rogare ut eos baculis repellerent.

# Augury

Like the ancient Greeks, the Romans laid great stress upon augury, the "science" of "taking the omens". They would not contemplate taking any important step until it was clear from the omens that the gods were in favour of it.

First of all, they would offer a sacrifice to some appropriate god or gods. For example, for an important family event, they would offer a sacrifice to their household gods, called the **Lares** and **Penates**, at the family shrine in the **atrium**; someone planning to go on a journey might offer a sacrifice to Mercury, a soldier going into battle a sacrifice to Mars or Mithras, a young man in love an offering to Venus or Fortuna. The Romans worshipped many gods, both native and foreign; all of them would have their own temples, each with a sacrificial altar outside in the open air.

A procession on its way to the altar to sacrifice a pig, a sheep and a bull. (Photograph, The Mansell Collection)

At home, the sacrifice could be small cakes, honey, cheese or fruit which would be burnt upon the altar; but, at a temple, an animal—a pig, a sheep or a bull—would be sacrificed.

In the latter case, once the animal had been killed, the vital organs—heart, liver and intestines—were inspected by the **haruspices** who claimed to be able to tell from the spots or marks on these organs whether the omens were favourable or not. If the omens were bad, the ordinary Roman simply put off the undertaking to another day. More sceptical Romans usually dismissed all this as mumbo-jumbo and, in fact, the Elder Cato said "How can one **haruspex** look at another without laughing?"

The most popular form of augury, "taking the auspices", can be described quite accurately as "bird-watching" (from **avis**, a bird, and **spectare**, to watch). The **auspex** based his predictions upon the number of birds seen at a particular time, the direction of flight, and so on. Astrology, dreams, thunder and lightning, and strange events of any kind were all taken very seriously by those engaged in augury.

# 52
# Papirius
# Praetextatus

Now that Marcus has assumed the **toga virilis**, Cornelius will begin to consider his public career. In the early Republic, boys began their training for public life when they were much younger than Marcus is now. In those days fathers took their sons with them while they carried out their public duties. This story shows that Papirius, though still wearing the **toga praetexta**, had already learned how to be discreet.

mos antea senatoribus Romae fuit in Curiam cum praetext-
atis filiis introire. olim in senatu res maior agebatur et in diem
posterum prolata est. placuit ne quis eam rem enuntiaret.
mater Papirii, pueri qui cum parente suo in Curia fuerat,
rogavit filium quid in senatu patres egissent. puer tamen
respondit non licere eam rem enuntiare. eo magis mulier audire
cupiebat; silentium pueri animum eius adeo incitavit ut vehem-
entius quaereret.

tum puer, matre urgente, prudens consilium cepit. dixit
actum esse in senatu utrum unus vir duas uxores haberet an una
uxor duos viros. hoc ubi illa audivit, domo trepidans egressa
est. ad ceteras matronas rem pertulit.

venit ad senatum postridie matronarum caterva. lacrimantes
atque obsecrantes oraverunt ut una uxor duos viros haberet
potius quam ut unus vir duas uxores. senatores ingredientes in
Curiam mirabantur quid matronae vellent.

puer Papirius in medium progressus narravit quid mater
audire cupivisset et quid ipse matri dixisset. senatus fidem atque
ingenium pueri laudavit ac consultum fecit ne postea pueri cum
patribus in Curiam introirent praeter illum unum Papirium.
puero postea cognomen honoris causa *Praetextatus* datum est
quod tantam prudentiam praebuerat.

**mos, moris** (*m*), custom
**posterus, -a, -um,** next, following
**placuit ne,** it was decided that . . . not
**enuntio** (1) to reveal, divulge
**patres, patrum** (*m.pl*), senators
**eo magis,** all the more
**dixit actum esse,** he said that there had been a debate
**utrum . . . an . . . ,** whether . . . or . . .

**trepidans, -antis,** in a panic
**potius quam,** rather than
**fides, fidei** (*f*), good faith, reliability
**ingenium, -i** (*n*), intelligence, ingenuity
**consultum, -i** (*n*), decree
**cognomen, cognominis** (*n*), nickname
**honoris causa,** as an honour
**praebeo** (2), to display, show

**ago, agere** (3), **egi, actum,** to discuss
**profero, proferre, protuli, prolatum,** to carry forward, continue
**urgeo, urgere** (2), **ursi,** to press, insist

# Roman Names

In the earliest days, most Romans had only two names, that of the clan or **gens** to which they belonged (**nomen**), and their personal name by which they would be addressed by relatives and friends (**praenomen**). Later, as families divided, branches of the same **gens** were distinguished by a third name (**cognomen**),

e.g. Gaius (personal name) **praenomen**
    Julius (name of **gens**) **nomen**
    Caesar (branch of Julian **gens**) **cognomen**

The **cognomen** frequently started off as a nickname given to one member of the family, and it was handed down to his descendants as part of their name even though the nickname did not apply to them personally,

e.g. P. Ovidius Naso ("big nose")
    L. Domitius Ahenobarbus ("bronze beard")
    M. Junius Brutus ("the stupid one")
    C. Licinius Calvus ("bald")

A few Romans, who had earned some special distinction, were granted a fourth name (**agnomen**) which was usually connected with the event which had made them famous,

e.g. Publius Cornelius Scipio, who conquered the Carthaginians in North Africa, was called Publius Cornelius Scipio Africanus.

Females were normally given the feminine form of the father's **nomen**, e.g. Cornelia is the daughter of Cornelius, and the daughter of M. Tullius Cicero was called Tullia.

It is usual in Latin books to find the **praenomen** abbreviated. This is not the same as our practice of giving someone's initials. In Latin each abbreviation stands for a particular name:

| | | | | | |
|---|---|---|---|---|---|
| App. | = Appius | L. | = Lucius | S(ex). | = Sextus |
| A. | = Aulus | M. | = Marcus | Sp. | = Spurius |
| C. | = Gaius | M'. | = Manius | T. | = Titus |
| Cn. | = Gnaeus | P. | = Publius | Ti(b). | = Tiberius |
| D. | = Decimus | Q. | = Quintus | | |

# Roman Weddings II

In spite of the unromantic pre-arrangements, the wedding itself was celebrated with great festivity by the families and guests. The second half of June was considered to be the luckiest time for a wedding.

On the evening before her marriage, the girl dedicated her toys to the household gods to show that her childhood had ended, just as a boy dedicated his **toga praetexta** and **bulla** at the coming-of-age ceremony. At the same time, she received her **mundus muliebris**—the jewellery, perfumes, toilet articles and attire of the grown-up woman.

On her wedding day the bride wore a **tunica recta** which was plain white and over it a cloak (**palla**) which was saffron-yellow, as were her sandals. Her hair was specially styled for the occasion, and over it she wore a bright orange veil (**flammeum**). Her attendant was a married woman (**pronuba**). The bride's house where the wedding ceremony (**nuptiae**) was performed was also decorated for the occasion.

The bride and her family and friends assembled in the atrium and received the bridegroom and his guests. The ceremony began with a sacrifice, usually of a pig, the entrails of which were carefully examined by the **auspex** to make sure that the omens were favourable. If they were unfavourable, the marriage was postponed. The ceremony also included the signing of the marriage contract (**tabulas nuptiales obsignare**) by ten witnesses, the joining of the couple's right hands (**dextras iungere**) by the **pronuba** and the repetition of the formula **ubi tu Gaius, ego Gaia** by the bride. Then the guests all shouted "Good Luck!" (**feliciter!**).

The ceremony was followed by a banquet and then, after nightfall, the couple prepared to go to their new home. The bridegroom pretended to carry off the bride by force just as the Romans once carried off the Sabine women. Then the bride and groom were escorted home by a procession of guests (**deductio**) carrying torches (**taedae**) and singing songs to Hymen, God of Marriage. Some guests threw nuts (**nuces**) to children for luck. On arrival at the house, the bride was carried over the threshold (**super limen tollere**) to avoid an unlucky stumble.

# 53
# Cornelia's Wedding

ubi dies nuptialis venit, omnes mature surrexerunt. Aurelia Marcum Sextumque hortabatur ut festinarent. ancillae huc illuc concursabant ut omnia pararent.

Flavia et Vinia, mater eius, iam diu aderant. mox adveniebant ceteri amici et propinqui. appropinquantes laeti viderunt ianuam et postes vittis et coronis myrti laurique ornatos esse. domum ingressi in atrium ducti sunt ubi Cornelia, tunicam albam induta, flammeum gerens, eos exspectabat. paulo post clamor risusque maximus auditus est. Valerius cum propinquis amicisque suis intrabat.

Cornelia cum pronuba ad aram stabat. sacris rite paratis, auspex processit ut porcum sacrificaret. deinde tabulae nuptiales obsignatae sunt. Vinia pronuba dextras Valerii et Corneliae iunxit. Valerio roganti "quid nomen tibi est?" Cornelia "ubi tu Gaius ego Gaia" respondit. quo facto, cuncti "feliciter!" exclamabant.

cena iam parata, omnes convivae accubuerunt, atque optimam post cenam consecuta est commissatio hilaritatis plena.

iam advesperascebat. Cornelia ad matrem haerebat; Valerius simulabat se eam e manibus matris vi abripere. mox illa ad domum novam magna caterva comitante deducebatur. praecedebant quinque pueri qui taedas ardentes ferebant; subsequebantur ceteri ridentes et cantantes; nuces ad liberos, qui undique concurrerant, coniciebant. cum ad domum venissent, nova nupta super limen sublata est ne laberetur.

"quam felix est Cornelia!" exclamavit Flavia.

**mature,** early
**vitta, -ae** ($f$), ribbon
**myrtus, -i** ($f$), myrtle
**laurus, -i** ($f$), bay (tree)
**orno** (1), to decorate
**paulo post,** a little later
**ara, -ae,** ($f$), altar

**sacer, sacra, sacrum,** sacred
**rite,** properly
**vi,** by force
**simulo** (1), to pretend
**ne laberetur,** in case she stumbled
**felix, felicis,** lucky

**iungo, iungere** (3), **iunxi, iunctum,** to join
**ardeo, ardere** (2), **arsi, arsum,** to burn
**nubo, nubere** (3), **nupsi, nuptum** ( + *dat.*), to marry

# PURPOSE CLAUSES

In addition to the uses of **ut** with the subjunctive described on page 56 (Result) and page 64 (Telling to), **ut** is used to express Purpose. Here, it is usually most naturally translated by *to* or *so that*. The negative **ne** can be translated in various ways, e.g. *so that ... not*; *in case*; *to avoid*; *to prevent*.

> e.g. auspex processit **ut** porcum **sacrificaret**.
> *The priest stepped forward* **to sacrifice** *a pig*.

> super limen sublata est **ne laberetur**.
> *She was carried over the threshold*
> **in case she stumbled.**
> **to prevent her from stumbling.**

Note that the verb in the purpose clause is in the subjunctive.

## Exercise 53a

*Translate:*
1  multi amici convenerunt ut novae nuptae gratularentur.
2  ianitor baculum habet ut clientes repellat.
3  Marcus ante Lararium stabat ut bullam Laribus consecraret.
4  cavete ne cadatis, amici!
5  ancilla in cubiculum festinavit ut Corneliae speculum daret.
6  servus vestimenta custodit ne quis ea surripiat.
7  Flavia Romam veniet ut Corneliam adiuvet.
8  Eucleides per vias festinavit ne a praedonibus caperetur.
9  pater Sexti Romam redibit ut filium secum domum ducat.
10 Marcus ad Tabularium deductus est ut nomen eius in tabulis publicis inscriberetur.

# Exercise 53b

## A Noble Wife

There is much evidence to show that husbands and wives loved each other and lived as happily as if they had themselves chosen each other. When a bride repeated the words **ubi tu Gaius ego Gaia** at the wedding ceremony, she was promising to be a faithful wife. The following story tells us how Arria, during the illness of her husband, concealed the death of her son from him to avoid aggravating his illness.

aegrotabat Caecina Paetus, maritus Arriae; aegrotabat et filius, uterque mortifere, ut videbatur. filius decessit, puer eximia pulchritudine et parentibus carissimus. huic Arria ita funus paravit, ita duxit exsequias ut ignoraret maritus. praeterea cum cubiculum eius intraverat, simulabat vivere filium atque etiam convalescere; ac Paeto saepe interroganti quid ageret puer, respondebat "bene quievit; libenter cibum sumpsit." deinde cum lacrimae prorumperent, e cubiculo egrediebatur. tum se dolori dabat. tandem siccis iam oculis, vultu iam composito redibat; atque dum maritus aegrotabat, sic lacrimas retinebat, dolorem operiebat.

**maritus, -i** (*m*), husband
**mortifere,** mortally, critically
**eximius, -a, -um,** outstanding
**carus, -a, -um,** dear, beloved
**funus, funeris** (*n*), funeral

**duxit exsequias,** (she) carried out the funeral rites
**cum,** whenever
**quid ageret,** how he was
**siccus, -a, -um,** dry

**decedo, decedere** (3), **decessi, decessum,** to die
**quiesco, quiescere** (3), **quievi, quietum,** to rest
**compono, componere** (3), **composui, compositum,** to compose
**operio, operire** (4), **operui, opertum,** to hide, cover

# Roman Funerals

When a death occurred in a Roman family, it was the custom to display grief more than is done in our country. Tears and lamentations were expected, and it was usual, for female mourners at least, to beat the breast (**pectus plangere**) and go about with torn clothing (**scissa veste**) and dishevelled hair (**capillis solutis**). Some families even hired professional mourners to do this for them.

In the case of an important family, like the Cornelii in our story, the actual funeral procession (**pompa**) was a very elaborate affair. After the body had lain in state, feet towards the door, in the atrium of the house surrounded by lamps (**lucernae**) and candles (**candelae**), there would be a procession through the city to the Forum and then on to the family tomb. It would be headed by trumpet players (**tubicines**) followed by the litter on which the body lay. Then, after professional mourners, singers of dirges (**neniae**) and torch-bearers (a reminder of the days when all funerals had taken place at night), came members of the family wearing masks of famous ancestors (**imagines maiorum**), and, in the case of a magistrate, even the public attendants (**lictores**) carrying his symbol of office (**fasces**). Family and friends followed. A halt was made in the Forum where a speech of praise (**laudatio**) was made in honour of the dead man.

At the family tomb outside the walls, the body was usually placed on a funeral pyre (**rogus**) which was set alight by a member of the family after some of the deceased's possessions had been placed on it. Flowers and spices were also thrown on the fire.

After the body had been cremated, the ashes were cooled with wine and were collected with the bones in an urn and placed in the family tomb. The last farewell was then uttered and after nine days of mourning a food offering was made at the tomb to the spirit of the dead man (**manes**).

Slaves and the very poor, who could not afford even to hire the four bearers to carry the bier, were usually buried in public cemeteries in simple coffins. Some, however, would join one of the guilds or societies that were formed to ensure a respectable funeral for their members and spare them the indignity of being flung into a common grave. The poor were buried on the day they died, and their funerals, like those of children, usually took place after dark with the minimum of ceremony. Death among children was common, both in the early vulnerable years and in later childhood, as is proved by many inscriptions found on tombstones in various parts of the Roman world, including Britain.

## Another Story about Arria

Arria's devotion is further illustrated by the following story:

Many years later, Scribonianus had taken up arms against Claudius in Illyria, and Paetus had taken part in the revolt. Scribonianus was killed, and Paetus was captured and put on board a ship to be taken to Rome. When he was about to go on board, Arria pleaded with the soldiers to be allowed to go with him. "Surely a man of senatorial rank is entitled to have some slaves to prepare his food, dress him and put on his shoes? I will do all of these tasks on my own." Her request was refused, however. She therefore hired a small fishing boat and followed the larger vessel. When they reached Rome, Paetus was condemned to death, but he was told that he might take his own life, if he wished. At that point, Arria, who had no desire to go on living after the death of her husband, drew a dagger, plunged it into her breast, drew it out and, as she held it out to her husband, she uttered the immortal words **Paete, non dolet** ("Paetus, it does not hurt").

Pliny, *III. 16*

# 54

# A Sad Occasion

mense Iulio tantus erat calor in urbe ut omnes ad villam redire vellent. Gaius Cornelius igitur omnia parare coepit ut Baias rediret. antequam profectus est, accidit res tristissima.

Cornelius, ut solebat, cum Tito fratre ad balneas iverat. per totam domum erat silentium. subito auditae sunt voces atque clamor. Cornelius servos hortabatur ut lecticam in domum maxima cum cura ferrent. Aurelia, vocibus auditis, in atrium irrupit. "quid factum est, Gai? cur servos iubes lecticam in domum ferre?" cui Cornelius "Titus noster aliquid mali accepit. frigidarii pavimentum tam leve et lubricum erat ut ille lapsus ceciderit. puto eum coxam fregisse. medicus statim est arcessendus."

multos dies Titus in lecto iacebat. primo convalescere videbatur; mox tamen fiebat infirmior, nam in febrem subito inciderat. in dies morbus ingravescebat.

tandem tam infirmus erat ut vix loqui posset. haud multo post e vita excessit. Cornelius maximo dolore affectus est. tota domus se dolori dedit. Aurelia et Cornelia et omnes ancillae, scissa veste capillisque solutis, pectora plangebant. corpus Titi, toga praetexta opertum, in atrio in lecto funebri positum est. circum lectum ardebant lucernae et candelae.

postridie corpus Titi summo honore elatum est. praecedebant tubicines. subsequebantur in pompa viri taedas tenentes, mulieres nenias cantantes, propinqui imagines maiorum gerentes, lictores fasces ferentes; postremi incedebant familiares.

cum in forum venissent, Gaius Cornelius processit ut fratrem mortuum laudaret. commemoravit qualis vir Titus fuisset, quot merita in principem civesque contulisset.

quo facto, corpus Titi ad sepulcra Viae Flaminiae in pompa latum est. ibi rogus exstructus erat. in rogum impositum est corpus et super corpus vestes atque ornamenta. appropinquavit Gaius Cornelius taedam manu tenens. quam taedam oculis aversis in rogum iniecit.

exsequiis confectis, Cornelii tristes domum regressi sunt. multa de Tito loquebantur. commemorabant quam hilaris fuisset, quantum liberos amavisset. "maxime" inquiunt "nos omnes eum desiderabimus."

**cura, -ae** ($f$), care  
**levis, -is, -e,** smooth  
**coxa, -ae** ($f$), hip bone  
**est arcessendus,** must be sent for  
**febris, febris** ($f$), fever  
**morbus, -i** ($m$), illness  

**funebris, -is, -e,** funeral  
**commemoro** ($1$), to mention, recount  
**merita conferre,** to render services (to)  
**hilaris, -is, -e,** cheerful  

**frango, frangere** ($3$), **fregi, fractum**, to break  
**ingravesco, ingravescere** ($3$), to grow worse  
**exstruo, exstruere** ($3$), **exstruxi, exstructum,** to build  

## The ending -sco

Verbs which end in **-sco** signify "grow" or "become", e.g.

**ingravesco,** I grow worse
**conticesco,** I become silent
**convalesco,** I grow well

**advesperascit,** it grows dark
**quiesco,** I grow quiet
**senesco,** I grow old

What do the following English words mean: convalescent, adolescent, efflorescent, crescent, incandescent?

# An Account of Roman Funerals

(as given by Polybius, a historian of the second century BC)

Whenever an important citizen dies, they have a funeral procession, in which his body is carried into the Forum to the Rostra, sometimes upright so as to be conspicuous, less often in a reclining position. There, surrounded by the whole populace, a grown-up son mounts the rostrum and delivers a speech about the virtues and achievements of the deceased. As a result, the majority of those present are so deeply affected that the loss seems not merely a private one affecting the relatives only, but a public loss involving everyone.

Then, after he is buried with the usual ceremonies, they place a likeness of the deceased in a part of the house where everyone can readily see it, and enclose it in a little wooden shrine. This likeness is a mask which reproduces with remarkable faithfulness the features and complexion of the deceased.

On the death of any important member of the family, these likenesses are taken to the Forum, worn by those members of the family who seem most nearly to resemble them in height and bearing. These people wear togas with a purple border if the deceased was a consul or praetor, totally purple if he was a censor, and edged with gold if he had celebrated a triumph or had any similar distinction. They all ride in chariots preceded by the **fasces,** axes and other emblems appropriate to the official positions held by each during his life; and when they arrive at the Rostra, they all sit down in their proper order on chairs of ivory.

It would be difficult to imagine a sight more inspiring to an ambitious young man than to see the likenesses of men who had once been famous for their goodness, all together and as if alive and breathing. What sight could be finer than this?

Besides, the person who makes the speech over the deceased, after speaking of the deceased himself, goes on to tell of the successful exploits of the other ancestors whose likenesses are present, beginning from the earliest. In this way, by constantly refreshing their memories about the fame of good men, the glory of those who performed noble deeds becomes immortal, and the fame of those who served their country well is passed on to future generations.

Polybius, *Histories VI. 3*

# Epitaphs

Roman tombs ranged from the very simple to the extremely elaborate. There was usually an inscription on the tomb and many of these have survived. The following four are in some cases slightly modified:

(a) Pontia Prima hic est sita. noli violare!

      **situs,** buried            **violare,** to do harm

(b) est hoc monumentum Marci Vergilei Eurysacis pistoris re- demptoris apparitoris.

      **pistor,** baker            **redemptor,** contractor
               **apparitor,** public servant

(c) Carfinia Marci liberta vixit annos XX. iucunda suis, gratissima amicis, omnibus officiosa fuit.

**iucundus,** a delight to     **gratus,** loved by
**officiosus,** ready to serve, obliging

(d) Dis Manibus. C. Tullius Hesper aram fecit sibi ubi ossa sua coniciantur. quae si quis violaverit aut inde exemerit, opto ei ut cum dolore corporis longo tempore vivat et, cum mortuus fuerit, inferi eum non recipiant.

**Dis Manibus,** to the spirits    **eximere,** to remove
of the dead                   **inferi,** gods of the
**optare,** to wish              underworld

(e) hospes, quod dico paullum est, adsta et perlege.
hic est sepulchrum haud pulchrum pulchrae feminae:
nomen parentes nominarunt Claudiam.
suum maritum corde dilexit suo:
natos duos creavit; horum alterum
in terra linquit, alium sub terra locat.
sermone lepido, tum autem incessu commodo
domum servavit. lanam fecit. dixi. abi.

**cor, cordis** (*n*), heart      **incessus, -us** (*m*), bearing
**natus, -i** (*m*), son          **commodus, -a, -um,**
**lepidus, -a, -um,**           dignified
    charming               **lana, -ae** (*f*), wool

**diligo, diligere** (3), **dilexi, dilectum,** to love
**linquo, linquere** (3), **liqui,** to leave

The following military epitaphs come from Britain and are shown as far as possible in their original form, with the full Latin version on the right:

(f) From Housesteads:

| | |
|---|---|
| D M | Dis Manibus |
| ANICIO | Anicio |
| INGENVO | Ingenuo, |
| MEDICO | medico |
| ORD COH | ordinario cohortis |
| I TVNGR | primae Tungrorum. |
| VIXIT ANN XXV | vixit annos viginti quinque. |

**ordinarius,** serving in      **Tungri, -orum** (*m.pl*),
   the ranks                  the Tungri, a Belgic tribe

(g) From York:

DM SIM PLICIAE·FLORENTINE
ANIM E·INNOCENTISSIME
QVE·VIXITM ENSESDECEM
FELICIVS·SIMPLEX·PATER·FECIT
L·EG·VI·V

Dis Manibus Simpliciae
Florentinae,
animae innocentissimae,
quae vixit menses decem,
Felicius Simplex, pater, fecit
legionis sextae Victricis.

**anima, -ae** (*f*), soul

**Victrix,** the Victorious
(the name of the
legion)

(h) From Colchester:

M FAVON M F POL FACI

LIS > LEG XX VERECVND

VS ET NOVICIVS LIB POSV
ERVNT H S E

Marcus Favonius, Marci
filius,
Pollia, Facilis, centurio
legionis
vicesimae (Verecundus et
Novicius, liberti, posuerunt)
hic situs est.

**Pollia (tribu),**
belonging to
the Pollian tribe

>, symbol which means
'centurion'

The epitaph of Marcus
Favonius. (Colchester and
Essex Museum)

# TRANSLATING ut

You have now met the following uses of **ut**:

## A. With an indicative verb:

>semper, ut vides, negotiosus sum.
>*As you see, I am always busy.*

>Sextus, ut lupum conspexit, arborem ascendit.
>*When Sextus caught sight of the wolf, he climbed the tree.*

Clue: **ut** followed by an indicative verb should be translated by *as* or *when*.

## B. With a subjunctive verb:

1 *Result*

>tam infirmus erat ut vix loqui posset.
>*He was so weak that he could scarcely speak.*

Clue: A word like **tam, tantus, talis, tot** or **adeo** suggests that the translation will be *so ... that.*

2 *"Telling to"*

>Cornelius servos hortabatur ut lecticam maxima cum cura ferrent.
>*Cornelius was urging the slaves to carry the litter very carefully.*

>oraverunt ut una uxor duos viros haberet.
>*They begged that one wife should have two husbands.*

Clue: The **ut** clause depends on a verb of "telling", "ordering", "begging", "urging", "persuading", etc.

This type of clause is sometimes called an *indirect command*.

3 *Purpose*

>Gaius Cornelius processit ut fratrem mortuum laudaret.
>*Gaius Cornelius came forward to praise his dead brother.*

This type of **ut** clause is very common after verbs which suggest that someone went somewhere *to do* something.

# Exercise 54a

What would you expect **ut** to mean in the following sentences?

1 Cornelius Corneliae praecepit ut . . . .
2 tantus erat terror in urbe ut . . . .
3 Marcus, ut vides, est filius senatoris.
4 ianitor servis imperavit ut . . . .
5 in urbem descendit ut . . . .
6 Aurelia tam irata erat ut . . . .
7 pueri ut vocem patris audiverunt . . . .
8 senatores nuntium miserunt ut . . . .
9 Sextus adeo esuriebat ut . . . .
10 Eucleides, ut nos omnes scimus, est eruditissimus.


# Exercise 54b

*Translate:*

1 magister Sexto imperavit ut domum statim rediret.
2 Sextus, ut imperaverat eius magister, domum statim rediit.
3 in balneis paulisper morabantur ut cum amicis colloquerentur.
4 pueri, ut Titum viderunt, eum laeti salutaverunt.
5 amico meo persuasi ut mecum ad Circum veniret.
6 Eucleides, ut vos omnes scitis, fabulas pueris semper narrare vult.
7 servo imperavi ut panem emeret.
8 Cornelii ex urbe Roma discedent ut Baias redeant.
9 Marcus nos rogat ut secum ad theatrum eamus.
10 Eucleides "ut feriati estis," inquit "vos moneo ut multos libros legatis."

# Funeral Customs

## Two Laws Concerning Burial

(a)  Law of the XII Tables:

> hominem mortuum in urbe ne sepelito neve urito.
> *No one must bury or burn a dead man in the city.*

(b)  Law of the Colony of Julia Genetiva in Spain:

> No person shall bring a dead person or bury one or
> burn one inside the boundaries of the town or the area
> marked round by the plough or build a monument to a
> dead person there. Any person breaking this law shall
> be fined 5000 sesterces.

## The Crier's Words at a Ceremonial Funeral

————*, a citizen, has died; it is now time for those for
whom it is convenient to go to his funeral. ————* is being
brought from his house for burial.

* name of deceased.

# Revision Exercise A

*Translate:*

1 scimus multos fures vestimenta e balneis surrepta in urbe vendere.
2 Pyramus, vestigiis leonis visis, putavit puellam necatam esse.
3 Thisbe, corpore Pyrami viso, gladio stricto ipsa se occidit.
4 ex urbe profecturi audivimus viam Appiam esse clausam. nunc nescimus quando Baias perventuri simus.
5 pueri ex atrio egredientes, voce~Eucleidis audita, in cubiculum confugere constituerunt.
6 Sextus speravit se suum patrem visurum esse. e ludo enim domum missus sciebat Cornelium se puniturum esse.
7 Tito roganti Cornelius respondit Aureliam ad amphitheatrum non ituram esse; eam domi manere malle.
8 Marcus Titum conspectum rogavit quot spectatores amphitheatro contineri possent.
9 gladiatores pugnaturi Caesarem salutare solent. sciunt multos esse morituros.
10 Galli urbem captam incenderunt; Romani se defendere non poterant.
11 Aurelia servos in culina loquentes audivit.
12 Cornelia Valerium ad Italiam regressum esse non audiverat.
13 spectatores non audiverant cur servus liberatus esset.
14 stirpe e pede extracta, leo recubuit et dormivit.
15 princeps, fabula audita, constituit servo parcere. negavit enim se umquam prius talem fabulam audivisse.
16 audivimus spectatores, cum leonem hominis manus lambentem vidissent, attonitos fuisse.
17 Cornelius putavit Titum domum se secutum esse; sed mox intellexit eum in amphitheatro moratum esse.
18 Sexto viso, fur effugere conans in pavimento lapsus est.
19 "eheu!" inquit Thisbe. "puto meum velamen te perdidisse." quibus verbis dictis, se occidere conata est.
20 iam pro certo habemus nos omnia intellegere.

    **nego** (1), to say that . . . not

# Revision Exercise B

*Translate:*

1. Cornelia tam defessa erat ut paene lacrimaret.
2. Cornelius Sextum monuit ne iterum in ludo tam ignavus esset.
3. ianitor eis imperabat ut statim abirent.
4. matronae ad senatum lacrimantes venerunt ut senatoribus persuaderent.
5. servus in aquam desiluit ne fur effugeret.
6. Eucleides pueris persuasit ut vera dicerent.
7. Cornelia nescit cur pater se adesse in tablino iusserit.
8. pueros rogavit ut extra tablinum manerent.
9. Gaius pueros monuit ne e cubiculo exirent.
10. ancillae in cubiculum festinaverunt ut crines Aureliae curarent.
11. servus arborem ascendit ne caperetur.
12. ille liber est talis ut Aurelia eum legere nolit.
13. tanta multitudo ad domum convenit ut omnibus intrare non liceret.
14. tam longum erat iter ut Valerius defessus esset.
15. Sextum Marcus rogavit ut sibi narraret quid in amphitheatro actum esset.
16. princeps imperavit ne servus occideretur.
17. cives in palaestram excedebant ut se exercerent.
18. Aeneas ad Hesperiam navigabat ut urbem novam conderet.
19. servus casam piratarum celerrime petivit ut dominum servaret.
20. grammaticus ferulam rapuit ut Sextum verberaret.
21. praedones tam celeriter cucurrerunt ut Eucleidem facile consequerentur.
22. tot et tanta erant incendia ut cives aedificia servare non possent.
23. tanta tempestas coorta est ut milites navem conscendere vix possent.
24. Eucleides Sexto imperavit ne pupam laederet.
25. Cornelia matrem rogavit ut servum arcesseret ut cum eo loqueretur.

# Vocabulary

## A

**a, ab** ( + *abl.*), by, from, away from

**abeo, -ire, -ii, -itum,** to go away

**abhinc** ( + *acc.*), ago

**abripio** (3), **-ripui, -reptum,** to snatch away

**ac,** and

**accidit** (3), **accidit,** to happen

**accipio** (3), **-cepi, -ceptum,** to receive, welcome

**accumbo** (3), **-cubui, -cubitum,** to recline (at table)

**acriter,** fiercely

**ad** ( + *acc.*), to, towards, at, near

**adeo,** so much, to such an extent

**adhuc,** still

**adiuvo** (1), **-iuvi, -iutum,** to help

**admiratio, -onis** ( *f* ), amazement

   **admiratione captus,** in utter amazement

   **admirationi esse,** to be a source of wonder or surprise

**admiror, -ari** (1), **-atus sum,** to wonder (at)

**admitto** (3), **-misi, -missum,** to commit (a crime)

**adstantes, -ium** (*m.pl*), bystanders

**adsto** (1), **-stiti,** to stand near, stand by

**adsum, adesse, adfui,** to be present, be near

**adulescens, -entis** (*m*), young man, youth

**advenio** (4), **-veni, -ventum,** to come to, reach, arrive at

**advesperascit** (3), **advesperavit,** evening is coming on, it is getting dark

**aedificium, -i** (*n*), building

**aedifico** (1), to build

**aeger, -gra, -grum,** ill

**aegroto** (1), to be ill

**affectus, -a, -um,** affected, moved

**affero, afferre, attuli, allatum,** to bring to, bring

**age! agite!,** come! come on!

**ager, agri** (*m*), field, territory, land

**ago, agere** (3), **egi, actum,** to do, drive, discuss, spend (time)

   **gratias agere** ( + *dat.*), to thank

   **agere de** ( + *abl.*), to discuss

**ait,** (he, she) says, said

**albus, -a, -um,** white

**alias,** at another time

**aliquis, aliquid,** someone, something

   **aliquid mali,** some harm

**alius, alia, aliud,** other, another, different

   **alii ... alii ...,** some ... others ...

**alter, altera, alterum,** the one, the other, the second

**ambo, ambae, ambo,** both

**ambulo** (1), to walk

**amica, -ae** ( *f* ), friend

**amicus, -i** (*m*), friend

**amo** (1), to like, love

**amor, amoris** (*m*), love

**amphitheatrum, -i** (*n*), amphitheatre

**amplector, -plecti** (3), **-plexus sum,** to embrace

**ancilla, -ae** ( *f* ), maidservant, servant-girl

**anima, -ae** ( *f* ), soul

**animus, -i** (*m*), mind, spirit, will
  **animum recuperare,** to
    recover one's senses
  **in animo habere,** to intend
  **bono animo es!** cheer up!
**annus, -i** (*m*), year
**ante** ( + *acc.*), before, in front of
**antea,** previously
**antequam,** before
**anulus, -i** (*m*), ring
**aperio** (4), **aperui, apertum,** to
  open
**apodyterium, -i** (*n*), changing
  room
**apparitor, -oris** (*m*), public
  servant
**appropinquo** ( 1 ) ( + *dat.*), to
  approach, draw near (to)
**apto** ( 1 ), to fit, place
**apud** ( + *acc.*), at the house of
**aqua, -ae** (*f*), water
**ara, -ae** (*f*), altar
**arbor, -oris** (*f*), tree
**arcesso** (3), **-ivi, -itum,** to
  summon, send for
**ardeo** (2), **arsi, arsum,** to burn,
  blaze
**arena, -ae** (*f*), arena, sand
**ascendo** (3), **ascendi,**
  **ascensum,** to climb
**aspergo** (3), **aspersi,**
  **aspersum,** to sprinkle, splash
**at,** but
**atque,** and
**atrium, -i** (*n*), atrium, main room
**attente,** attentively
**attonitus, -a, -um,** astonished,
  astounded
**audio** (4), **-ivi, -itum,** to hear,
  listen to
**aufugio** (3), **-fugi,** to run away
**aureus, -a, -um,** golden
**auspex, auspicis** (*m*), augur,
  officiating priest
**aut,** or
  **aut ... aut ...,** either ... or ...

**autem,** however, but, moreover
**auxilium, -i** (*n*), help
**ave! avete!,** hail!
**averto** (3), **averti, aversum,** to
  turn away, divert
**avis, avis** (*f*), bird

## B

**baculum, -i** (*n*), stick
**Baiae, -arum** (*f.pl*), Baiae
**balneae, -arum** (*f.pl*), baths
**bene,** well
**benevolentia, -ae** (*f*), kindness
**bestia, -ae** (*f*), beast
**bestiarius, -a, -um,** involving
  wild beasts
**blande,** in a friendly way
**bonus, -a, -um,** good
  **bono animo es!** cheer up!
**bos, bovis** (*m/f*), ox, cow
**brevis, -is, -e,** short
  **brevi tempore,** in a short time
**Britanni, -orum** (*m.pl*), Britons
**Britannia, -ae** (*f*), Britain
**bulla, -ae** (*f*), luck-charm, locket

## C

**cado** (3), **cecidi, casum,** to fall
**caelum, -i** (*n*), heaven, sky
**caldarium, -i** (*n*), hot-room (at
  baths)
**calor, -oris** (*m*), heat
**calvus, -a, -um,** bald
**candela, -ae** (*f*), candle
**canto** ( 1 ), to sing
**capillatus, -a, -um,** with long
  hair
**capilli, -orum** (*m.pl*), hair
  **capillis solutis,** with
    dishevelled hair
**capio** (3), **cepi, captum,** to take,
  capture, adopt (a plan)
**caput, capitis** (*n*), head
**carus, -a, -um,** dear
**casa, -ae** (*f*), hut
**caterva, -ae** (*f*), crowd

**cauda, -ae** (*f*), tail
**caupo, -onis** (*m*), innkeeper
**causa, -ae** (*f*), cause, reason
  *genitive* + **causa,** for the sake of
**cavea, -ae** (*f*), cage
**caveo** (2), **cavi, cautum,** to
  beware
**celeritas, -atis** (*f*), speed
  **summa celeritate,** with the
    utmost speed, at top speed
**celeriter,** quickly
  **quam celerrime,** as quickly as
    possible
**celo** (1), to hide, conceal
**cena, -ae** (*f*), dinner
**ceno** (1), to dine
**certe,** certainly, at least
**certus, -a, -um,** certain
  **pro certo habere,** to be sure
**ceteri, -ae, -a,** the rest
**cibus, -i** (*m*), food
**circum** ( + *acc.*), round, round
  about
**circumspicio** (3), **-spexi,**
  **-spectum,** to look around
**Circus, -i** (*m*), the Circus
  Maximus
**cista, -ae** (*f*), chest, trunk
**civis, -is** (*m*), citizen
**clamo** (1), to shout
**clamor, -oris** (*m*), shout,
  shouting
**claudo** (3), **clausi, clausum,** to
  shut, close
**claudus, -a, -um,** lame
**clementer,** quietly, gently
**cliens, clientis** (*m*), client,
  dependant
**coepi,** I began
**cogito** (1), to think, consider
**cognomen, -inis** (*n*), nickname
**cognosco** (3), **cognovi,**
  **cognitum,** to find out, learn,
  hear of
**cogo** (3), **coegi, coactum,** to
  force, compel

**collis, -is** (*m*), hill
**colloquor, -loqui** (3),
  **collocutus sum,** to speak
  together, converse
**comitor, -ari** (1), **-atus sum,** to
  accompany
**commemoro** (1), to mention,
  recount
**commissatio, -onis** (*f*),
  drinking party
**committo** (3), **-misi, -missum,**
  to entrust
  **pugnam committere,** to join
    battle
**commodus, -a, -um,** dignified
**commotus, -a, -um,** moved,
  excited
  **ira commotus,** becoming
    angry, in a rage
**communis, -is, -e,** common
**compleo** (2), **-plevi, -pletum,** to
  fill, complete
**complures, -es, -a,** several
**compono** (3), **-posui, -positum,**
  to compose
**concrepo** (1), **-crepui,** to snap
  (fingers)
**concurro** (3), **-curri, -cursum,**
  to run together, rush up
**concurso** (1), to rush about, run
  to and fro
**condemno** (1), to condemn
**condo** (3), **condidi, conditum,**
  to found, establish
**(merita) confero, -ferre,**
  **contuli, collatum,** to render
  (services)
**conficio** (3), **-feci, -fectum,** to
  finish
**confugio** (3), **-fugi,** to flee for
  refuge
**congredior, -gredi** (3),
  **-gressus sum,** to come
  together
**conicio** (3), **-ieci, -iectum,** to
  throw

**conor, -ari** (1), **-atus sum,** to try
**conscendo** (3), **-scendi,**
  **-scensum,** to board (ship)
**consecro** (1), to dedicate
**consensus, -us** (*m*), agreement
**consequor, -sequi** (3), **-secutus**
  **sum,** to catch up, overtake
**consido** (3), **-sedi, -sessum,** to
  sit down
**consilium, -i** (*n*), plan
**consisto** (3), **-stiti,** to halt, stop,
  stand
**conspicio** (3), **-spexi,**
  **-spectum,** to catch sight of
**constat,** it is agreed
**constituo** (3), **-stitui,**
  **-stitutum,** to decide
**consultum, -i** (*n*), decree
**conticesco** (3), **-ticui,** to fall
  silent
**contineo** (2), **-tinui, -tentum,** to
  confine, hold
**contra** ( + *acc.*), opposite, in front
  of
**convalesco** (3), **-valui,** to grow
  stronger, get well
**convenio** (4), **-veni, -ventum,** to
  come together, meet, assemble
**converto** (3), **-verti, -versum,**
  to turn, turn round
**conviva, -ae** (*m*), guest (at
  banquet)
**coorior, -iri** (4), **coortus sum,**
  to rise up, arise
**cor, cordis** (*n*), heart
**cornicen, -inis** (*m*), horn-player,
  bugler
**corona, -ae** (*f*), garland, crown
**corpus, corporis** (*n*), body
**cotidie,** daily, every day
**coxa, -ae** (*f*), hip-bone
**cras,** tomorrow
**credo** (3), **credidi, creditum**
  ( + *dat.*), to believe
**creo** (1), to appoint
**crinis, -is** (*m*), hair

**crudelis, -is, -e,** cruel
**crudelitas, -atis** (*f*), cruelty
**cubiculum, -i,** (*n*), bedroom
**cui,** dative of **qui, quae, quod**
**culina, -ae** (*f*), kitchen
**cum** ( + *abl.*), with
**cum,** when, since, whenever
  **cum primum,** as soon as
**cuncti, -ae, -a,** all
**cupio** (3), **-ivi -itum,** to wish,
  desire
**cur?,** why?
**cura, -ae** (*f*), care
  **curae esse,** to be a cause of
    anxiety
**Curia, -ae** (*f*), Senate House
**curo** (1), to look after, attend to
**curro** (3), **cucurri, cursum,** to
  run
**custodio** (4), to guard
**custos, -odis** (*m*), guard

## D

**de** ( + *abl.*), down from, about,
  concerning
**decedo** (3), **-cessi, -cessum,** to
  die
**decet** ( + *acc.*), (someone) should
**deditus, -a, -um,** devoted,
  dedicated
**deduco** (3), **-duxi, -ductum,** to
  show into, bring, escort
**deductio, -onis** (*f*), procession
**defendo** (3), **defendi,**
  **defensum,** to defend
**defessus, -a, -um,** weary, tired
**defrico** (1), **-fricui, -frictum,** to
  rub down
**deinde,** then
**delecto** (1), to delight
**deleo** (2), **-evi, -etum,** to destroy
**deliciae, -arum** (*f.pl*), delight
**demissus, -a, -um,** downcast
**depello** (3), **-puli, -pulsum,** to
  drive on to, drive ashore
**depono** (3), **-posui, -positum,**

to lay down, put aside

**descendo** (3), **-scendi,
-scensum,** to climb down

**desidero** (1), to long for

**desilio** (4), **-silui, -sultum,** to
leap down

**despondeo** (2), **-spondi,
-sponsum,** to promise, betroth

**deus, -i** (*m*), (*dat.pl.* **dis**), god
**di immortales!,** good
heavens!
**di manes,** the spirits of the
dead

**devoro** (1), to devour

**dextra, -ae** (*f*), right hand

**dico** (3), **dixi, dictum,** to say, tell

**dies, diei** (*m*), day
**in dies,** every day, daily
**dies natalis,** birthday

**digitus, -i** (*m*), finger
**digitis micare,** to play **morra**

**diligenter,** carefully

**diligo** (3), **dilexi, dilectum,** to
love

**dimitto** (3), **-misi, -missum,** to
send away, let go

**discedo** (3), **-cessi, -cessum,** to
depart, leave, go away

**diu,** for a long time

**dives, divitis,** rich

**do** (1), **dedi, datum,** to give
**dono dare,** to give as a gift

**doceo** (2), **docui, doctum,** to
teach

**doleo** (2), to grieve, be sad

**dolor, -oris** (*m*), grief, pain

**dominus, -i** (*m*), master

**domus, -us** (*f*), house, home
**domi,** at home

**dormio** (4), to sleep

**dos, dotis** (*f*), dowry

**duco** (3), **duxi, ductum,** to lead,
take
**exsequias ducere,** to carry
out funeral rites

**dum,** while

**duo, duae, duo,** two

**dux, ducis** (*m*), general, leader

## E

**e, ex** ( + *abl.*), out of, from

**ecce!,** look! behold!

**educo** (3), **eduxi, eductum,** to
lead out

**effugio** (3), **-fugi,** to escape

**ego,** I

**egredior, -i** (3), **egressus sum,**
to go out, leave, disembark

**eheu!,** alas!

**emo** (3), **emi, emptum,** to buy

**enim,** for

**enuntio** (1), to reveal, divulge

**eo, ire, ivi, itum,** to go

**eo,** there, to that place

**eo magis,** all the more

**epistola, -ae** (*f*), letter

**epulae, -arum** (*f.pl*), banquet,
feast

**erga** ( + *acc.*), towards

**eruditus, -a, -um,** learned,
scholarly

**esurio** (4), to be hungry

**et,** and, also

**etiam,** also, even

**euge!** hurray!

**evado** (3), **evasi, evasum,** to
escape

**exanimatus** (**metu**), paralysed
(with fear)

**excedo** (3), **-cessi, -cessum,** to
go out, leave
**e vita excedere,** to die

**excito** (1), to stir up, excite,
waken

**exclamo** (1), to shout out

**exeo, -ire, -ii, -itum,** to go out

**exerceo** (2), to exercise, train

**eximius, -a, -um,** outstanding

**eximo** (3), **-emi, -emptum,** to
remove

**exprimo** (3), **-pressi,
-pressum,** to express

**exsequiae, -arum** (*f.pl*), funeral rites

**exsilio** (4), **exsilui,** to leap out

**exspecto** (1), to wait for, await

**exstruo** (3), **-struxi, -structum,** to build

**extra** ( + *acc.*), outside

**extraho** (3), **-traxi, -tractum,** to drag out, draw out

**exuo** (3), **exui, exutum,** to take off

### F

**fabula, -ae** (*f*), story

**facile,** easily

**facio** (3), **feci, factum,** to make, do

**familia, -ae** (*f*), family, household

**familiares, -ium** (*m.pl*), close friends

**familiaris, -is, -e,** (belonging to the) family, household

**fasces, -ium** (*m.pl*), rods (symbol of office)

**febris, -is** (*f*), fever

**feliciter!** good luck!

**felix, felicis,** happy, lucky, fortunate

**femina, -ae** (*f*), woman

**fere,** almost, approximately

**feriatus, -a, -um,** on holiday

**fero, ferre, tuli, latum,** to carry, bring

**ferociter,** fiercely

**ferox, ferocis,** fierce

**ferula, -ae** (*f*), cane

**festino** (1), to hurry

**fides, -ei** (*f*), good faith, reliability

**filia, -ae** (*f*), daughter

**filius, -i** (*m*), son

**fio, fieri, factus sum,** to be done, made, happen

**flammeum, -i** (*n*), orange (bridal) veil

**follis, -is** (*m*), bag

**fortasse,** perhaps

**forte,** perchance, by chance

**fortis, -is, -e,** brave

**fortiter,** bravely

**forum, -i** (*n*), forum, market-place

**frango** (3), **fregi, fractum,** to break

**frater, fratris** (*m*), brother

**frigidarium, -i** (*n*), cold room (at baths)

**frigidus, -a, -um,** cold

**frustra,** in vain

**fugio** (3), **fugi, fugitum,** to flee

**funebris, -is, -e,** funeral

**funus, funeris** (*n*), funeral

**fur, furis** (*m*), thief

**furor, -oris** (*m*), frenzy

**furtim,** stealthily

### G

**Galli, -orum** (*m.pl*), Gauls

**Gallia, -ae** (*f*), Gaul

**gaudeo** (2), **gavisus sum,** to rejoice

**gemo** (3), **-ui, -itum,** to groan

**gens, gentis** (*f*), family, clan

**genus, -eris** (*n*), kind, race

**gero** (3), **gessi, gestum,** to wear, carry on

**gladiator, -oris** (*m*), gladiator

**gladius, -i** (*m*), sword

**gradior, -i** (3), **gressus sum,** to go

**grammaticus, -i** (*m*), teacher

**gratias agere** ( + *dat*), to thank

**gratulor, -ari** (1), **-atus sum** ( + *dat*), to congratulate

**gratus, -a, -um,** pleasing, dear (to), loved (by)

**gravis, -is, -e,** heavy, serious

### H

**habeo** (2), to have, hold

**habito** (1), to live, dwell

**haereo** (2), **haesi, haesum,** to stick, cling

**harpastum, -i** (*n*), ball game, hand ball
**haruspex, -icis** (*m*), soothsayer
**haud,** not
**heri,** yesterday
**heus!,** ho there!
**hic, haec, hoc,** this
**hic,** here
**hilaris, -is, -e,** cheerful
**hilaritas, -atis** (*f*), good humour, merriment
**hodie,** today
**homo, -inis** (*m*), man, fellow
**homines, -um** (*m.pl*), people
**honoris causa,** as an honour
**hora, -ae** (*f*), hour
**hortor, -ari** (1), **-atus sum,** to encourage, urge
**hospes, -itis** (*m*), friend, guest
**huc,** here, hither
**huc illuc,** here and there, hither and thither
**humanus, -a, -um,** human
**humi,** on the ground

# I

**iaceo** (2), to lie
**iam,** now, already
**ianitor, -oris** (*m*), doorkeeper
**ianua, -ae** (*f*), door
**ibi,** there
**id quod,** (a thing) which
**idem, eadem, idem,** the same
**igitur,** therefore
**ignavus, -a, -um,** lazy
**ignoro** (1), to be ignorant, not to know
**ille, illa, illud,** that; he, she, it
**illuc,** there, to that place
**imago, imaginis** (*f*), likeness, mask
**immanis, -is, -e,** huge
**immitto** (3), **-misi, -missum,** to hurl at, hurl into, let loose
**immortalis, -is, -e,** immortal
**impero** (1) ( + *dat.*), to order

**impetus, -us** (*m*), attack
**impono** (3), **-posui, -positum,** to place on, put
**in** ( + *abl.*), in, on
**in** ( + *acc*), into, towards
**in dies,** daily, every day
**incedo** (3), **-cessi, -cessum,** to march, go
**incendium, -i** (*n*), fire
**incendo** (3), **incendi, incensum,** to burn, set on fire
**incessus, -us** (*m*), bearing
**incido** (3), **incidi, incasum,** to fall into (on to)
**incipio** (3), **incepi, inceptum,** to begin
**incito** (1), to drive on, rouse
**incola, -ae** (*m*), inhabitant
**inde,** from there
**induo** (3), **indui, indutum,** to put on
**ineo, inire, inii, initum,** to go in, enter
**inferi, -orum** (*m.pl*), gods of the underworld
**infirmus, -a, -um,** shaky, disabled
**ingenium, -i** (*n*), intelligence, ingenuity
**ingens, -entis,** huge, great
**ingravesco** (3), to grow worse
**ingredior, -i** (3), **ingressus sum,** to go into, enter
**inicio** (3), **inieci, iniectum,** to throw into, thrust
**inquit,** he (she) says, said
**inscius, -a, -um,** not knowing
**inscribo** (3), **-scripsi, -scriptum,** to write in, register
**instructus, -a, -um,** drawn up
**intellego** (3), **-exi, -ectum,** to understand, realise
**inter** ( + *acc.*), between, among
**interpello** (1), to interrupt
**interrogo** (1), to ask
**intro** (1), to enter

**introduco** (3), **-duxi, -ductum,** to bring in

**introeo, -ire, -ii, -itum,** to enter

**invenio** (4), **-veni, -ventum,** to find

**invito** (1), to invite

**invitus, -a, -um,** unwilling(ly)

**iocus, -i** (*m*), joke, funny story

**ipse, ipsa, ipsum,** -self

**ira, -ae** (*f*), anger
   **ira commotus,** becoming angry, in a rage

**iracundus, -a, -um,** irritable, in a bad mood

**iratus, -a, -um,** angry

**irrumpo** (3), **-rupi, -ruptum,** to burst in, attack

**is, ea, id,** that; he, she, it
   **id quod,** (a thing) which

**ita,** thus, in this way
   **ita vero!** yes!

**Italia, -ae** (*f*), Italy

**itaque,** and so, therefore

**iter, itineris** (*n*), route, journey, way

**iterum,** again, a second time

**iubeo** (2), **iussi, iussum,** to order

**iucundus, -a, -um,** pleasant, a delight

**Iudaeus, -i** (*m*), Jew

**iugulo** (1), to kill, murder

**iungo** (3), **iunxi, iunctum,** to join

**iuvenis, -is** (*m*), young man

### L

**labor, labi** (3), **lapsus sum,** to slip, stumble

**laboro** (1), to work

**lacrima, -ae** (*f*), tear

**lacrimo** (1), to weep, cry

**laedo** (3), **laesi, laesum,** to harm

**laete,** joyfully

**laetus, -a, -um,** joyful, happy

**lambo** (3), **lambi,** to lick

**lana, -ae** (*f*), wool

**lanista, -ae** (*m*), trainer

**lararium, -i** (*n*), shrine of household gods

**Lares, -um** (*m.pl*), household gods

**lateo** (2), to lie in hiding, hide

**latrunculus, -i** (*m*), robber; (*pl*) pawns (a game like chess)

**laudatio, -onis** (*f*), speech of praise, eulogy

**laudo** (1), to praise

**laurus, -i** (*f*), bay tree, laurel

**lavo** (1), **lavi, lautum** or **lavatum** or **lotum,** to wash

**lectica, -ae** (*f*), litter

**lectus, -i** (*m*), bed

**lego** (3), **legi, lectum,** to read

**lente,** slowly

**leo, leonis** (*m*), lion

**lepidus, -a, -um,** charming

**levis, -is, -e,** smooth

**libenter,** gladly

**Liberalia, -ium** (*n.pl*), the Liberalia (Festival of Liber)

**liberi, -orum** (*m.pl*), children

**libero** (1), to set free

**libertus, -i** (*m*), freedman

**licet** (2), **licuit** ( + *dat.*), it is allowed

**lictor, -oris** (*m*), lictor, officer

**limen, -inis** (*n*), threshold, doorway

**lingua, -ae** (*f*), tongue, language

**linquo** (3), **liqui,** to leave

**linteum, -i** (*n*), towel

**loco** (1), to place

**locus, -i** (*m*), place

**longus, -a, -um,** long

**loquor, -i** (3), **locutus sum,** to speak

**lubricus, -a, -um,** slippery

**lucerna, -ae** (*f*), lamp

**lucet** (2), **luxit,** it is daylight

**luctor, -ari** (1), **-atus sum,** to wrestle

**ludo** (3), **lusi, lusum,** to play
**ludus, -i** (*m*), game, school
**lupus, -i** (*m*), wolf
**lux, lucis** (*f*), light
  **prima luce,** at dawn

## M

**magister, -tri** (*m*), teacher,
  schoolmaster
**magistratus, -us** (*m*), magistrate
**magnus, -a, -um,** big, great
**maior, -oris,** greater
  **maiores, -um** (*m.pl*), ancestors
**malo, malle, malui,** to prefer
**malus, -a, -um,** bad, evil
**mane,** in the morning, early
**maneo** (2), **mansi, mansum,** to
  remain
**manes, -ium** (*m.pl*), spirits of the
  dead
**mansuetus, -a, -um,** tame
**manus, -us** (*f*), hand, band
**mappa, -ae** (*f*), napkin
**maritus, -i** (*m*), husband
**mater, matris** (*f*), mother
**matrimonium, -i** (*n*), marriage
  **in matrimonium ducere,** to
    marry
**matrona, -ae** (*f*), married
  woman
**mature,** early
**maxime,** very, very much, most
**maximus, -a, -um,** greatest, very
  great
**mecum,** with me
**medicus, -i** (*m*), doctor
**medius, -a, -um,** mid-, middle of
**mehercule!** by Hercules! my
  goodness!
**memorabilis, -is, -e,** memorable
**mensis, -is** (*m*), month
**mercator, -oris** (*m*), merchant
**meridiani, -orum** (*m.pl*), mid-
  day fighters
**meridies, -ei** (*m*), noon, mid-day

**meritum, -i** (*n*), good deed,
  (*pl*) services
**metus, -us** (*m*), fear
**meus, -a, -um,** my
**mico** (1), **-ui,** to move quickly to
  and fro, flash
  **digitis micare,** to play **morra**
**miles, -itis** (*m*), soldier
**mille,** thousand
**minime,** least; no!
**minuo** (3), **-ui, -utum,** to lessen,
  reduce
**minus,** less
**mirabilis, -is, -e,** wonderful
**miror, -ari** (1), **-atus sum,** to
  wonder
**mirus, -a, -um,** wonderful
**miser, -a, -um,** wretched,
  unhappy
**mitis, -is, -e,** gentle
**mitto** (3), **misi, missum,** to
  send
**modus, -i** (*m*), way, method
**molestus, -a, -um,** troublesome,
  annoying
**moneo** (2), to advise, warn
**monumentum, -i** (*n*),
  monument, tomb
**morbus, -i** (*m*), illness
**morior, -i** (3), **mortuus sum,** to
  die
**moror, -ari** (1), **-atus sum,** to
  delay, remain
**mortifere,** fatally, critically
**mortuus, -a, -um,** dead
**mos, moris** (*m*), custom
**moveo** (2), **movi, motum,** to
  move
**mox,** soon
**muliebris, -is, -e,** womanly,
  female, of a woman
**mulier, -eris** (*f*), woman
**multitudo, -inis** (*f*), crowd
**multus, -a, -um,** much;
  (*pl*) many
**mundus, -i** (*m*), world, universe

**munus, -eris** (*n*), gladiatorial show; (*pl*) games
**murus, -i** (*m*), wall
**musso** (1), to mutter
**mutuus, -a, -um,** mutual, common, of each other
**myrtus, -i** (*f*), myrtle

# N

**nam,** for
**narro** (1), to tell (a story)
**natalis, -is, -e,** (belonging to) birth
**natura, -ae** (*f*), nature
**natus, -i** (*m*), son
**navigo** (1), to sail
**navis, -is** (*f*), ship
**-ne,** (indicates a question)
**ne** (+ *subjunctive*), in case, to prevent, not to
**ne ... quidem,** not even
**nec,** and ... not
    **nec ... nec ...,** neither ... nor ...:
**neco** (1), to kill
**neglego** (3), **-exi, -ectum,** to neglect, ignore
**nego** (1), to say ... not
**negotiosus, -a, -um,** busy
**nemo,** no one
**nenia, -ae** (*f*), lament, dirge
**neque,** and ... not
    **neque ... neque ...,** neither ... nor ...
**nescio** (4), to be ignorant, not to know
**nihil,** nothing
**nil,** nothing
**nobilis, -is, -e,** noble
**noctu,** by night
**noli** (+ *infin.*), do not ...
**nolo, nolle, nolui,** to be unwilling, refuse
**nomen, -inis** (*n*), name
**nomino** (1), to name, call by name

**non,** not
**nondum,** not yet
**nonne,** (asks a question expecting answer "yes")
**nonnulli, -ae, -a,** some
**nonus, -a, -um,** ninth
**nos,** we, us
**noster, -tra, -trum,** our
**novem,** nine
**novus, -a, -um,** new
**nox, noctis** (*f*), night
**nubo** (3), **nupsi, nuptum** (+ *dat.*), to marry
**nullus, -a, -um,** no, none
**num?,** surely ... not?
**numquam,** never
**nunc,** now
**nuntius, -i** (*m*), messenger
**nuper,** recently
**nupta, -ae** (*f*), bride
**nuptiae, -arum** (*f.pl*), wedding ceremony
**nuptialis, -is, -e,** wedding (*adj.*)
**nux, nucis** (*f*), nut

# O

**obsecro** (1), to beg, beseech
**observo** (1), to watch
**obsigno** (1), to sign
**obstupefactus, -a, -um,** astounded
**occido** (3), **-cidi, -cisum,** to kill
**occupatus, -a, -um,** busy
**octo,** eight
**oculus, -i** (*m*), eye
**officiosus, -a, -um,** ready to serve, obliging
**officium, -i** (*n*), official ceremony
**olim,** once upon a time, one day
**omnis, -is, -e,** all, every
**operio** (4), **-ui, opertum,** to hide, cover
**oportet te** (+ *infin.*), you must
**optimus, -a, -um,** best, excellent, very good
**opto** (1), to wish

**ordinarius, -a, -um,** serving in the ranks

**ornamentum, -i** (*n*), decoration

**orno** (1), to decorate, equip

**oro** (1), to beg

**os, oris** (*n*), mouth, face

**os, ossis** (*n*), bone

**osculum, -i** (*n*), kiss

**ostendo** (3), **-di, ostentum,** to show, point out

## P

**paedagogus, -i** (*m*), tutor

**paene,** almost

**palaestra, -ae** (*f*), exercise-ground

**palla, -ae** (*f*), cloak

**palus, -i** (*m*), post

**panis, -is** (*m*), bread
　**panem et circenses,** bread (dole) and circus shows

**par impar,** odds or evens (a game)

**parco** (3), **peperci, parsum** ( + *dat.*), to spare

**parens, -entis** (*m/f*), parent

**pareo** (2) ( + *dat.*), to obey

**paria, -ium** (*n.pl*), pairs

**paro** (1), to prepare

**pars, partis** (*f*), part

**parvus, -a, -um,** small

**pater, patris** (*m*), father
　**patres, -um** (*m.pl*), senators

**patior, pati** (3), **passus sum,** to suffer, endure

**patruus, -i** (*m*), uncle

**pauci, -ae, -a,** few

**paulisper,** for a short time

**paulo post,** a little later

**paulum,** a little, little

**pavimentum, -i** (*n*), tiled floor

**pectus, -oris** (*n*), chest, breast
　**pectus plangere,** to beat the breast

**pecunia, -ae,** (*f*), money

**per,** ( + *acc.*), through, along, over

**perdo** (3), **-didi, -ditum,** to destroy

**perfero, -ferre, -tuli, -latum,** to report

**periculum, -i** (*n*), danger

**peristylium, -i** (*n*), peristyle

**perlego** (3), **-legi, -lectum,** to read through

**persuadeo** (2), **-suasi, -suasum** ( + *dat.*), to persuade

**perterritus, -a, -um,** terrified

**perturbatus, -a, -um,** confused, embarrassed

**pervenio** (3), **-veni, -ventum** (**ad** + *acc.*), to reach, arrive (at)

**pes, pedis** (*m*), foot

**pessimus, -a, -um,** worst

**peto** (3), **-ivi, -itum,** to seek, make for, attack

**pila, -ae** (*f*), ball

**pilum, -i** (*n*), javelin

**pirata, -ae** (*m*), pirate

**pistor, -oris** (*m*), baker

**placeo** (2), ( + *dat.*), to please

**placide,** quietly, tamely

**placuit ne,** it was decided that . . . not

**plenus, -a, -um,** full

**pluit,** it rains

**plurimus, -a, -um,** very much, most

**plus,** more

**pompa, -ae** (*f*), funeral procession

**pono** (3), **posui, positum,** to place, put

**popina, -ae** (*f*), eating-house, snack-bar

**populus, -i** (*m*), people

**porcus, -i** (*m*), pig

**porta, -ae** (*f*), gate

**porto** (1), to carry

**posco** (3), **poposci,** to ask for, demand

**possum, posse, potui,** to be able

**post** ( + *acc.*), after

**post,** after, later

**postea,** afterwards

**posterus, -a, -um,** next, following

**postis, -is** (*m*), doorpost

**postremo,** finally

**postremus, -a, -um,** last

**postridie,** on the next day

**potius quam,** rather than

**praebeo** (2), to show, display, provide

**praecedo** (3), **-cessi, -cessum,** to go in front

**praecipio** (3), **-cepi, -ceptum** (+ *dat.*), to instruct, order

**praeclarus, -a, -um,** famous

**praedo, -onis** (*m*), robber

**praenomen, -inis** (*n*), forename

**praeter** (+ *acc.*), except

**praeterea,** besides, moreover

**praetextatus, -a, -um,** wearing the **toga praetexta**

**prehendo** (3), **-endi, -ensum,** to seize

**primo,** at first, first

**primum,** first

**primus, -a, -um,** first
  **prima lux,** dawn

**princeps, -cipis** (*m*), emperor, leading citizen

**prior, -oris,** first, previous

**prius,** previously

**pro di immortales!** good heavens!

**procedo** (3), **-cessi, -cessum,** to step forward

**procul,** far, far off

**profero, -ferre, -tuli, -latum,** to carry forward, continue

**proficiscor, -i** (3), **profectus sum,** to set out

**progredior, -i** (3), **-gressus sum,** to go forward, advance

**pronuba, -ae** (*f*), bride's attendant

**prope** (+ *acc.*), near

**propinquus, -i** (*m*), relative

**propter** (+ *acc.*), on account of

**prorumpo** (3), **-rupi, -ruptum,** to burst forth, burst out

**prudens, -entis,** sensible, wise

**prudentia, -ae** (*f*), good sense, discretion, skill

**publicus, -a, -um,** public

**puella, -ae** (*f*), girl

**puer, -i** (*m*), boy

**puerilis, -is, -e,** childish, of childhood

**pugna, -ae** (*f*), battle
  **pugnam committere,** to join battle

**pugno** (1), to fight

**pulcher, -chra, -chrum,** beautiful

**pulchritudo, -inis** (*f*), beauty

**pulvinar, -aris** (*n*), imperial seat (at games)

**punio** (4), to punish

**pupa, -ae** (*f*), doll

**purus, -a, -um,** clean, plain white

**puto** (1), to think

# Q

**quadrans, -antis** (*m*), smallest Roman coin ($\frac{1}{4}$ of an **as**)

**quaero** (3), **quaesivi, quaesitum,** to ask, look for

**quam!** how!

**quam,** than

**quamquam,** although

**quando?** when?

**quantus, -a, -um?** how big? how much?

**quasi,** as if

**-que,** and

**qui, quae, quod,** who, which

**quidam, quaedam, quoddam,** a, a certain; (*pl*) some

**quidem,** indeed
  **ne ... quidem,** not even

**quiesco** (3), **quievi, quietum,** to rest

**quinque,** five
**quintus, -a, -um,** fifth
**quis? quid?** who? what? which?
  **si quis,** if anyone
**quo?** where . . . to?
**quo . . . eo . . . ,** the (more) . . . the
  (more) . . .
**quod,** because
**quomodo?** how?
**quoniam,** since
**quoque,** also
**quot?** how many?
**quotus, -a, -um?** which (in
  numerical order)?

# R

**rapio** (3), **rapui, raptum,** to
  snatch, seize
**recitatio, -onis** (*f*), public
  reading
**recognitio, -onis** (*f*),
  recognition
**recumbo** (3), **-cubui,** to lie down
**reddo** (3), **reddidi, redditum,**
  to give back, return
**redemptor, -oris** (*m*), contractor
**redeo, -ire, -ii, -itum,** to go
  back, return
**reduco** (3), **-duxi, -ductum,** to
  lead back, take back
**refero, referre, rettuli,**
  **relatum,** to bring back
**regredior, -i** (3), **-gressus sum,**
  to go back, return
**relinquo** (3), **-liqui, -lictum,**
  to leave
**repello** (3), **reppuli, repulsum,**
  to drive back, beat back
**repeto** (3), **-petivi, -petitum,** to
  fetch, recover
**reprehendo** (3), **-hendi,**
  **-hensum,** to scold, reprimand
**res, rei** (*f*), thing, matter, affair,
  situation
  **res urbanae,** city affairs
**rescribo** (3), **-scripsi,**
  **-scriptum,** to write back, reply

**reservatus, -a, -um,** reserved
**resisto** (3), **restiti** ( + *dat.*), to
  resist
**respondeo** (2), **-spondi,**
  **-sponsum,** to reply
**retiarius, -i** (*m*), a net-fighter
**retineo** (2), **-tinui, -tentum,** to
  hold back
**re vera,** really
**rideo** (2), **risi, risum,** to laugh,
  laugh at
**ridiculus, -a, -um,** absurd,
  laughable
**rima, -ae** (*f*), crack
**risus, -us** (*m*), laughter, laugh,
  smile
**rite,** properly
**rixor, -ari** (1), **-atus sum,** to
  quarrel
**rogo** (1), to ask
**rogus, -i** (*m*), funeral pyre
**Roma, -ae** (*f*), Rome
**Romanus, -a, -um,** Roman
**rumpo** (3), **rupi, ruptum,** to break, burst
**rursus,** again
**russatus, -a, -um,** red

# S

**sacer, sacra, sacrum,** sacred,
  holy
**sacra, -orum** (*n.pl*), sacrifice
**sacrifico** (1), to sacrifice
**saepe,** often
**saevus, -a, -um,** fierce, savage
**saluto** (1), to greet, welcome
**salve! salvete!** good day!
  greetings! welcome!
**sanguineus, -a, -um,**
  bloodstained
**sanguis, -inis** (*m*), blood
**satis,** enough
**scelus, sceleris** (*n*), crime
**scio** (4), to know
**scissa veste,** with torn clothing
**scribo** (3), **scripsi, scriptum,**
  to write

**se,** himself, herself, itself, themselves

**secreto,** secretly

**secum,** with him (her, it, them)

**sed,** but

**sedecim,** sixteen

**sedeo** (2), **sedi, sessum,** to sit

**sella, -ae** (*f*), seat

**semper,** always

**senator, -oris** (*m*), senator

**senatus, -us** (*m*), senate

**senex, senis** (*m*), old man

**sentio** (4), **sensi, sensum,** to feel, notice, realise

**sepelio** (4), **-ivi, sepultum,** to bury

**sepulcrum, -i** (*n*), tomb

**sequor, -i** (3), **secutus sum,** to follow

**serenus, -a, -um,** clear, bright

**sermo, -onis** (*m*), conversation, talk

**sero,** late

**serva, -ae** (*f*), female slave

**servo** (1), to save, keep, protect

**servus, -i** (*m*), slave

**sex,** six

**sextus, -a, -um,** sixth

**si,** if

**si quis,** if anyone

**sic,** thus, in this way

**siccus, -a, -um,** dry

**silentium, -i** (*n*), silence

**silva, -ae** (*f*), wood

**similis, -is, -e,** like

**simul,** at the same time

**simulo** (1), to pretend

**sine** ( + *abl.*), without

**sine dubio,** without doubt

**sinister, -tra, -trum,** left

**sinistra, -ae** (*f*), left hand

**situs, -a, -um,** placed, buried

**sol, solis** (*m*), sun

**soleo** (2), **solitus sum,** to be accustomed

**solitudo, -inis** (*f*), loneliness, solitude

**solus, -a, -um,** alone

**somnus, -i** (*m*), sleep

**soror, -oris** (*f*), sister

**spectaculum, -i** (*n*), sight, spectacle

**spectator, -oris** (*m*), spectator

**specto** (1), to look at, watch

**speculum, -i** (*n*), mirror

**spelunca, -ae** (*f*), cave

**spero** (1), to hope

**spondeo** (2), **spopondi, sponsum,** to promise solemnly, pledge

**sponsa, -ae** (*f*), betrothed woman, bride

**sponsalia, -ium** (*n.pl*), betrothal

**sponsus, -i** (*m*), betrothed man, bridegroom

**statim,** immediately

**stirps, stirpis** (*f*), thorn

**sto** (1), **steti, statum,** to stand

**strepitus, -us** (*m*), noise, din, clattering

**strigilis, -is** (*f*), strigil, scraper

**stringo** (3), **strinxi, strictum,** to draw (a sword)

**stultus, -a, -um,** stupid, foolish

**stupeo** (2), to be amazed, gape

**sub** ( + *abl.*), under

**subito,** suddenly

**submissus, -a, -um,** quiet, subdued, soft

**subsequor, -i** (3), **-secutus sum,** to follow up

**summus, -a, -um,** the greatest, the top of . . .

**sumo** (3), **sumpsi, sumptum,** to take, pick up, assume, put on

**super** ( + *acc.*), above

**supero** (1), to overcome, defeat

**surgo** (3), **surrexi, surrectum,** to rise, get up

**surripio** (3), **-ripui, -reptum,** to steal

**suus, -a, -um,** his, her, its, their

## T

**tablinum, -i** (*n*), study (room)
**tabulae, -arum** (*f.pl*), records
**Tabularium, -i** (*n*), Public
  Records Office
**taceo** (2), to be silent
**taeda, -ae** (*f*), torch
**taedet,** it bores
  **me taedet** ( + *gen.*), I am bored
  (with), tired (of)
**talis, -is, -e,** such, of such a kind
**tam,** so
**tamen,** however
**tandem,** at length
**tantum,** so much
**tantus, -a, -um,** so great
**temerarius, -a, -um,** rash,
  reckless, bold
**tempestas, -atis** (*f*), storm
**templum, -i** (*n*), temple
**tempus, -oris** (*n*), time
**teneo** (2), **-ui, tentum,** to hold
**tepidarium, -i** (*n*), warm room
  (at baths)
**tergeo** (2), **tersi, tersum,** to dry,
  wipe
**terra, -ae** (*f*), earth
**terror, -oris** (*m*), terror
**tertius, -a, -um,** third
**tessera, -ae** (*f*), ticket
**theatrum, -i** (*n*), theatre
**thermae, -arum** (*f.pl*), public
  baths
**tigris, -is** (*m/f*), tiger
**timeo** (2), to fear
**timide,** fearfully, timidly
**timidus, -a, -um,** fearful, timid
**timor, -oris** (*m*), fear
**toga, -ae** (*f*), toga
  **toga praetexta,** toga with
    purple edging
  **toga pura,** plain white toga
  **toga virilis,** toga worn by
    adult male (plain white)

**tollo** (3), **sustuli, sublatum,** to
  lift, raise
**tot,** so many
**totus, -a, -um,** whole of
**trado** (3), **tradidi, traditum,** to
  hand over
**traho** (3), **traxi, tractum,** to drag
**transgredior** (3), **-i, -gressus**
  **sum,** to cross
**tremo** (3), **-ui,** to tremble
**trepidans, -antis,** in a panic
**tres, tres, tria,** three
**trigon, -onis** (*m*), ball game
  involving three people
**tristis, -is, -e,** sad
**tu,** you
**tubicen, -inis** (*m*), trumpet-
  player
**tum,** then, at that moment
**tumultus, -us** (*m*), uproar,
  commotion
**tunica, -ae** (*f*), tunic
**turba, -ae** (*f*), crowd
**tuus, -a, -um,** your

## U

**ubi?** where?
**ubi,** when
**una,** together
**unde?** where . . . from?
**undique,** from all sides
**unguentum, -i** (*n*), ointment,
  perfume
**unguo** (3), **unxi, unctum,** to
  anoint, smear with oil
**unus, -a, -um,** one
**urbanus, -a, -um,** of the city
  **res urbanae,** city affairs
**urbs, urbis** (*f*), city
**urgeo** (2), **ursi,** to press, insist
**ut** ( + *indic.*), when, as
**ut** ( + *subj.*), so that, that, to
**uterque, utraque, utrumque,**
  each (of two), both
**utrum . . . an . . . ?** whether . . . or
  . . . ?

**uxor, -oris** (*f*), wife

## V

**valde,** very, very much
**vale! valete!** goodbye
**valedico** (3), **-dixi, -dictum,** to say goodbye, bid farewell
**valeo** (2), to be strong, be well
**vapor, -oris** (*m*), steam
**varius, -a, -um,** different, various, varied
**vehementer,** violently, furiously, insistently
**vel,** or
   **vel ... vel ...,** either ... or ...
**velamen, -inis** (*n*), shawl, veil, head-scarf
**velle,** to wish
**venatio, -onis** (*f*), hunting, animal hunt
**vendo** (3), **-didi, -ditum,** to sell
**venio** (4), **veni, ventum,** to come
**ventus, -i** (*m*), wind
**verbero** (1), to beat
**verbosus, -a, -um,** talkative
**verbum, -i** (*n*), word
**vero,** truly
   **ita vero!** yes!
   **minime vero!** no!
**verus, -a, -um,** true
**vescor, -i** (3) ( + *abl.*) to feed (on)
**vester, -tra, -trum,** your
**vestibulum, -i** (*n*), entrance, passage
**vestigium, -i** (*n*), trace, footprint
**vestimenta, -orum** (*n.pl*), clothes

**vestis, -is** (*f*), clothing
**veto** (1), **-ui, -itum,** to forbid, tell not to
**vexo** (1), to annoy, tease
**via, -ae** (*f*), road, street
**viator, -oris** (*m*), traveller
**vicinus, -a, -um,** neighbouring
**Victrix, -icis,** the Victorious (name of a legion)
**video** (2), **vidi, visum,** to see
**videor, -eri** (2), **visus sum,** to seem
**villa, -ae** (*f*), country house, farm
**vinco** (3), **vici, victum,** to conquer, overcome
**vinum, -i** (*n*), wine
**violo** (1), to do harm to
**vir, -i** (*m*), man
**virgo, -ginis** (*f*), maiden
**virilis, -is, -e,** a man's, of a man
**vis, vim** (*acc.*), **vi** (*abl.*) (*f*), force
**vita, -ae** (*f*), life
**vitta, -ae** (*f*), ribbon, headband
**vivo** (3), **vixi, victum,** to live
**vix,** scarcely, with difficulty
**volo, velle, volui,** to wish, want
**vos,** you (*pl.*)
**vox, vocis** (*f*), voice
   **submissa voce,** in a subdued voice
**vulnero** (1), to wound
**vulnus, -eris** (*n*), wound
**vultus, -us** (*m*), face, expression
   **vultu demisso,** with eyes lowered